Show Me . . . Natural Wonders

by
Don Corrigan

with illustrations by E. J. Thias

REEDY PRESS
St. Louis, Missouri

Reedy Press
PO Box 5131
St. Louis, MO 63139
USA

Library of Congress Control Number: 2007921412

ISBN: 978-1-933370-13-2
          1-933370-13-0

For all information on all Reedy Press publications visit our website at www.reedypress.com.

Printed in the United States of America
07 08 09 10 11 5 4 3 2 1

Cover image: Castlewood's Meramec Bluffs, watercolor, E. J. Thias

design by Ellie Jones, MathisJones Communications

DEDICATION

The author and the artist wish to dedicate this book to every friend of nature who has ever taken the time to remove a beer can, fast-food wrapper or empty Cheetos bag from a precious outdoor site. The newts, crayfish and daddy longlegs cannot thank you for your efforts, so please allow us to intercede on their behalf.

In Memory of

Lorraine Williams

Given by the

Lorraine Williams

Memorial

CONTENTS

Caves and Caverns 111

Just Special Places 155

PREFACE

As a youngster, Samuel Clemens—later known as Mark Twain—reveled in the natural wonders of his home state of Missouri. He played an outlaw in its forests; he played an explorer in its caves; he played pirate and adventurer along its muddy creeks and its mighty river—the Mississippi.

As a storyteller, the great natural wonders of his youth became an integral part in Twain's tales of Tom Sawyer and Huckleberry Finn. The natural landscapes—hills, valleys, caves and streams—provided Twain with a refuge in his youth and an inspiration in his later years. And here's a little secret—those Show Me State natural wonders still exist. The wonders are still here to be explored, enjoyed—and protected.

This book is the result of a series of special moments in nature. One of those moments happened to me on a day trip to Twain's hometown of Hannibal. From the wooded slope of Cardiff Hill, with its climb to the famous hilltop lighthouse, this adventurer gazed south over the "white town drowsing." On the southern edge of the city stands another bluff, popularly known as "Lover's Leap."

It's there that a young Mark Twain witnessed a local religious sect, the Millerites, ascend to the bluff late one evening. They had donned robes and gowns and fully expected to be delivered to heaven from this lofty perch. Alas, when the sun rose up the next morning, the disappointed Millerites remained earthbound.

Twain reported that both the town and the religious in their robes felt a little bit humiliated. It's a great story, but why should there have been any sense of embarrassment?

There is nothing wrong with seeking an escape, some kind of transcendence, a sort of deliverance by visiting a special natural place. Perhaps the mistake of the Millerites was in their certitude of what the site would bring them. Surely, learning took place on that Hannibal bluff. Wisdom was imparted and taken away, if not exactly the knowledge of the eternal which the discouraged Millerites had hoped to attain.

This book is all about climbing bluff tops and fording streams—excitedly and without embarrassment—in search of the special moment, the unexpected enlightenment. *Show Me . . . Natural Wonders* is an escape manual—a guidebook to natural havens away from the stress of career demands, information overload and multitasking lifestyles.

Although a wide assortment of travel guides are already available to help with journeys to selected sites in the heartland, this book takes a different approach. It's designed as a guide on how to uniquely experience a natural setting: how to encounter it; how to think about it; how to meditate upon the meaning of place.

The book is divided into four sections. Section I is a compendium of exceptional bluffs, from the Weston Bluffs overlooking the Missouri River north of Kansas City to the limestone cliffs north of Cape Girardeau, which tower over a wide stretch of Mississippi River. Many more bluffs have been selected for their vistas and for other aesthetic considerations from within the interior of the state of Missouri.

Launched from these high places are flights of imagination. Imagine the travails of the Cherokee in their Trail of Tears march below the bluffs near Cape Girardeau. Imagine the anguish of the Nez Perce held captive at Ft. Leavenworth below the Weston Bluffs north of Kansas City.

Imagine meditations on these mounts in an effort to atone for blighted pasts or to seek out brighter futures.

Springs, streams and unusual water features are the focus of Section II of this portfolio of natural wonders. Playful prose and detailed pencil sketches bring to visual and aural life the cascading waters of Joplin's Grand Falls, the tearful streams of Mina Sauk or the chasm flows of the Castor River Shut-ins.

Quieter places chronicled include the brilliant Ozark Blue Spring off the Current River or the gorgeous Alley Spring with its bright green watercress, feathery ferns and flowery columbine. Water sites are meant to cleanse the soul or calm emotions. As noted in this volume, water sites can only perform such magic when they are protected from unnatural degradation.

It's impossible to do justice to Missouri's natural wonders without a section on the state's great wilderness underground. Section III of *Show Me . . . Natural Wonders* gives unique perspectives on well-known show caves in the state, as well as introducing nature enthusiasts to lesser-known underground marvels.

Caverns and cavescapes are among nature's greatest teachers. They give us insights into the beauty below the surface of things. They instruct us on the relationship between soft, living organisms and inert, petrified stone. They yield secrets about the hidden water flows that give us the light of life, and yet there is no more absolute darkness than that found in a cave.

Many of Missouri's natural wonders are not so easily classified as bluff, spring or cavern. Section IV is titled, "Just Special Places," and features popular nature trails, restored wetlands, boulder piles, unusual forests and more.

A tall-tale's reading accompanies the impressive illustration for Big Oak Tree State Park in the Missouri Bootheel, while Native American mythology is retold for sites such as Devil's Toll Gate. Adventurers are advised to watch out for the strange beasts inhabiting Allred Lake Cyprus Swamp. This remnant of Louisiana bayou is as primordial as it gets in the Show Me State.

Show Me . . . Natural Wonders invites readers to find, to frequent, and to discover joy in their very own special places. Contemplation is great and is a necessary salve for mind and body, but enjoyment of natural wonders should not always be a passive experience or a spectator sport.

One of the book's missions is to inspire folks to get active. Take a hike in the wondrous, natural asset of Roger Pryor Forest. Try out a mountain bike on the popular Chubb Trail above the Meramec River. Grab a paddle and enjoy the Vilander Bluffs or the Devil's Elbow Bluffs or Cardareva

Bluffs while canoeing Missouri's many fine rivers. The book provides an appendix of clearly explained directions on how to find and enjoy the Show Me State's natural wonders.

One cautionary note: an aspect of this volume that may give a reader pause is a kind of lackadaisical quality. The book is geographically—and thematically—all over the map.

Is it a book about the geological makeup of some special places? Is it a book about the local history of selected sites? Is it a book about recreational opportunities across the state? Is it a book of nostalgia, of things remembered about past visits to natural wonders? Is it a New Age consideration of earth's varied forms?

Actually, it's a smattering of all these things. Nature is diverse, and it evokes a myriad of responses. Nature and geography are especially diverse in Missouri, where the landforms of the Bootheel, the Ozark Mountains and the plains north of the Missouri River all differ dramatically from one another.

So, too, do these treatments of Show Me State natural wonders. They draw on waves of energy that differ from site to site. Sometimes that energy manifests itself in the history which occurred at a location; other times it can be as elemental as a locale's ancient geology. In all cases, it is all about the spirit of place—a spirit that evokes natural wonder. Historical energy animates the story of Arrow Rock, where a bluff home became an artist's residence. It is here that George Caleb Bingham framed within his brain the visions of life on the Missouri River flowing below and brought those visions to reality with a palette of bright colors.

Geological mystery permeates a profile of Hughes Mountain with its chimney-like rock formations from the pre-Cambrian period—more than a billion years ago. The odd, tightly packed aggregations of small rock columns inspired the site's initial trailblazers to aptly describe it as the "Devil's Honeycomb." What mad stonemason from an ancient past was at work here?

Nostalgia's indomitable voice comes through in the retelling of a camping trip of long ago to Castor River Shut-ins. Privileged guests of this natural haven will never forget the night when a full moon withdrew in a lunar eclipse. Insects were silenced and only the river Castor continued to babble in the darkness. On a canyon horizon, lightning bolts were seen to spar in the distance.

Native American folklore becomes a metaphorical string in an extended yarn about the Current River stop at Round Spring. Osage tribal folklore holds that a strong young brave caused the spring's cavern roof to collapse. Angered by his companions' insults, he beat the ground with his war club until the cave-in resulted.

Environmentalism's critical moral imperative becomes a compelling theme in the story of the conservation of Greer Spring. Formed by the convergence of three underground rivers, the ground virtually rumbles with its 222 million gallons of flowing icy water. A commercial enterprise proposed for the spring eventually gave way to a conservation effort. At a time when environmental victories are rare, here is one to savor.

Environmental literacy can no longer be described as an avocation or an altruistic, academic pursuit. It's a form of literacy that now appears essential to the survival of the human species, never mind those "lower life forms" which are being extinguished as you read these word strings.

Environmental literacy can be described as a basic understanding of ecosystems; as an appreciation for the various methods to nurture nature; as an ethical sense of responsibility to become good stewards of whatever small portion of the planet we happen to inhabit.

Environmental literacy can be fostered in any number of ways. Obviously, this treatise is biased toward the field trip—toward visiting natural wonders—as opposed to primarily classroom endeavors. The quest to retrieve nature from the brink inevitably requires a simple rediscovery of nature. That is a big part of what this book is all about.

Show Me . . . Natural Wonders offers several examples of folks who are rediscovering nature in order to retrieve it. In suburban St. Louis, a small city and a local school have teamed up to save, succor and sustain a 13-acre oasis of flora and fauna, forest and prairie. A high school teacher uses the tiny park to teach his students conservation techniques and environmental responsibility.

In Kansas City, volunteers with Blue River Rescue wade through the waters of a sullied urban stream. They pull out cans, bottles, tires, stoves, refrigerators, dumpsters and abandoned autos. Blue River Rescue volunteers number 900, and they have retrieved as much as 220 tons of trash in a year from the river they are intent on saving—convinced it can be a natural wonder.

"It's very satisfying to be a part of the effort to help the river," says Vicki Richmond of Blue River Rescue. "It's not just a matter of restoring a wild place; it raises ethical questions about how we live. And the river rescue creates a sense of ownership, you don't want other people jacking with your river."

ACKNOWLEDGMENTS

As the primary supplier of verbiage for this effort, it seems appropriate here to acknowledge the artistic contributions of my colleague, Ed Thias.

One of my favorite memories in the creation of this book will be our nature trail hikes and the aftermath—our breakfast discussions. On a morning after our hike to the bluffs of Emmenegger Park in the Kirkwood area of suburban St. Louis, Ed showed up for a breakfast meeting with photos, vertical and horizontal pencil drawings, and nature site paintings in water colors. He is a prodigious artist and talker—only a fraction of his work from this project appears in the book. His wife Doris helped a great deal with the drawings.

Other acknowledgments must include the production folks at Reedy Press; Carol Hemphill, a reading instructor at St. Louis Community College at Meramec, for her work in proofreading the text; my colleagues at the *Webster-Kirkwood Times* for their long-suffering patience with my extracurricular activities; and my colleagues at Webster University, who are always supportive.

Additional thanks is extended to my family. My wife Susanne and children, Brandon and Christa, were sometimes enlisted in my exploratory hikes, even though they did not always share my enthusiasm. My late uncle Stanley McCarron took me to many of the Ozark sites when I was a young boy and spurred my interest in the outdoors. His contribution to this book is seminal.

The students in my environmental journalism classes at Webster University also have been an inspiration for this book. Some of whom I must single out: Kara Beightal, Lindy Bunte, Leslie Cantu, Andrea Noble, Dale Hallett, Rachel Horne, Jon Kleinow, James Chilton, Jan Corzine, Stephanie Cunningham, Andy Dierker, Tiffany Johnson, Ryan Martin, Melanie Johnson, Brian Stuckmeyer, Alexandra Smith, Melanie Nitzsche, Deena Watts, Angie Zielinski, Latreecia Wade, Elizabeth Prusaczyk, Amy Swanson, Kara Price and Kerry McMahon.

Additional moral support came from the Environmental Studies Committee of Webster University: Jih-un Kim, Don Morse, Don Conway-Long, David Wilson, Art Sandler, J. C. Depew, Stephanie Schroeder, Allan McNeill, Karla Armbruster, Kim Kleinman, Ted Green and Kate Parsons.

Section I Unique Bluffs & Overlooks

Special thanks for assistance with Section I of this book go to Stan McTaggart and Scott Isringhausen with the Illinois Department of Natural Resources (DNR). They helped with information about southern Illinois bluffs that face Missouri. Charlie Hoessle of the St. Louis Zoo provided interesting wildlife stories about Illinois bluffs, such as those at Fults, which are frequently visited by Missourians.

Of course, officials with Missouri's DNR and the State Department of

Conservation also assisted with much of the book. Tour guides and park rangers were helpful at state parks and with the St. Louis County Parks and Recreation Department. Tourism officials and chambers of commerce were helpful with locations such as Rocheport, Arrow Rock and Hannibal.

Professors and public information specialists with several Missouri universities agreed to interviews. Carolyn Elwess, archivist at Park University, assisted with details on the Steamship *Arabia* and the Park promontory site. Steve Johnson of Benedictine College helped with information about the Benedictine Bluffs and the Missouri River Valley in western Missouri.

Section II Streams and Springs

Among those who assisted with Section II of the book were such groups as the Nature Conservancy, Sierra Club and Audubon Society. The Audubon Society was especially helpful with background on wildlife and wetlands.

Kay Drey with the Missouri Coalition for the Environment provided information on Ozark sites, as did John Karel of the L-A-D Foundation and Kathleen Henry of the Great Rivers Environmental Law Center. Another one of my favorite organizations, as a resource and for good works, is Trailnet of St. Louis. The Great Rivers Greenway District also should be singled out.

Canoe renters in the Ozarks provided useful background and stories. The Beletz brothers with the now-defunct Meramec River Canoe Club also proved to be great storytellers. Activist Roger Taylor with the coalition in support of the Missouri Scenic Rivers Act also provided assistance.

The skullers of the St. Louis Rowing Club were helpful with information about Creve Coeur Lake and with general water recreation in Missouri.

Don Ranley, my writing professor at the University of Missouri School of Journalism, has provided ideas and encouragement since I left Mizzou. Tom Shoberg of Pittsburg State University in Kansas provided geological information on southwest Missouri and Grand Falls.

Section III Caves and Caverns

Among those who assisted with Section III of the book were such groups as the the Meramec Valley Grotto, Missouri Speleological Survey, Missouri Caves Association and the Missouri Cave and Karst Conservancy.

Particularly helpful in explaining the cave hobby were Jim Ruedin and Jo Schaper of the Meramec Valley Grotto. Jonathon Beard of 3M Company provided background on caves in the Springfield area and his work on cave restoration. Scott House, who works with the Cave Research Foundation, assisted with information on southeast Missouri caves as well as caves in the Ozark Scenic Waterways area.

Special thanks to scuba diver Ole Van Goor who introduced me to the Bonne Terre Mine and West End Diving, which provided information on the old mine known as the Billion Gallon Lake Resort. The late Joe Wood of the now-defunct *St. Louis Globe-Democrat* related hours of stories about Meramec Caverns and other caves of the Meramec Valley.

Guides for both state park and commercial caves were extremely helpful for the cave section of the book. Special thanks to the Missouri Press Association and the Branson Chamber of Commerce for facilitating informational tours into caves in southwestern Missouri.

A former *Webster-Kirkwood Times* news intern, Anna Kopp, worked at the Onondaga State Park as a guide in 2005 and provided this writer with customized tours of caves in that area. She also facilitated interviews with other state park employees familiar with Missouri's many caves and bluffs.

Section IV Just Special Places

Nature Centers of the Missouri Department of Conservation have always been favorite destinations for me. Folks at the state locations in Springfield, Blue Spring and suburban St. Louis were invaluable.

Holly Berthold, Mike Arduser and Tamie Yegge, whom I've worked with at the Powder Valley Nature Center, have been especially helpful. A long-ago Halloween activity at Powder Valley was the genesis for one of the site profiles in Section IV.

Devotees of the late environmental activist Roger Pryor provided information on Grand Gulf, Greer Spring, the Roger Pryor Pioneer Backcountry and more. Those sources included members of the Missouri Coalition for the Environment and the L-A-D Foundation.

Sue Gustafson and Linda Tossing with the Important Bird Area (IBA) program of Audubon were especially helpful on the new Little Creve Coeur Wetlands in west St. Louis County. Jim Ziebol, Dennis Bozzay and Yvonne Homeyer, members of the St. Louis chapter of the North American Butterfly Association, provided information on butterfly habitats.

As always, state park officials were forthcoming with information about such sites as Pickle Springs, Big Oak Tree State Park, Route 66 State Park and more. St. Louis County's Lindbergh School District and the city of Sunset Hills, which jointly maintain Claire Gemp Park, provided details about the park's ecology.

Although this book is heavy on nature sites on the eastern side of the state, an effort was made to visit and experience locations in the Kansas City area. This could not have been accomplished without the help of Linda Lehrbaum of Kansas City Wildlands. Her organization put me in touch with Wildlands members and ecological restoration workers for a number of sites, including Blue River Rescue and other Kansas City area outdoors groups.

SHOW ME . . . NATURAL WONDERS

E.J.Thias

Unique Bluffs & Overlooks I

Bluffs come in all shapes and sizes. Some bluffs are framed by gently rising slopes on either side, which make them easily accessible. Other bluffs stand in a towering line with sheer faces, which make them formidable climbing exercises.

Bluffs are constructed with a variety of materials: hard granite and unrelenting rhyolite, uncertain shale and limestone, fine conglomerate mixes of sandstone, dirt and pebble. Bluffs may appear as crumbling stacks of uneven hot cakes or as stern walls of metamorphic rock.

All of this bluff diversity points to the magic of nature as architect. The attraction to this natural work seems ingrained in the DNA architecture of those with an affection for bluffs. This love of bluffs certainly seemed to be part of the biology—almost an instinctual urge—among my boyhood buddies.

From an early age, we walked the Southern Railway tracks to get to formations known as "Eagle's Nest" and what we referred to simply as the "Railroad Bluffs." These high spots were located between Edgemont Hill and the Shrine of Our Lady of the Snows, just west of Belleville, Ill.

Our adventures transpired before state governments spent much money on hiking trails to nature spots and tall bluffs. Railroad police frequently tried to discourage our rail hikes when we were youngsters, and I certainly discourage such treks now that I am older and wiser.

A perilous moment I will always remember involved a quick scramble up a bluff face as a freight train was approaching. A young fellow by the name of Don Rigney pulled me up one of those sheer bluffs by the arms, just as a string of locomotives rumbled through our secluded playground and shook the ground below us.

Atop the bluffs, we could watch the locomotives, the swaying freight cars and caboose disappear on their way to rail yards in East St. Louis. In the distance was a setting orange ball shining through the skyline of St. Louis, a gleaming city anchored on high land across the Mississippi River. The panoramic view of that western horizon was worth all our foolishness and the peril of the climb.

Later in life, "bluff love" brought about camping trips to the cliff caves of Fults in southern Illinois as well as eagle adventures to the north at Pere Marquette. And, of course, now bluff love has brought about this book, *Show Me . . . Natural Wonders.*

Fellow bluff lovers should be impressed with the cliff collection gathered in this volume. Included here are bluffs with interesting histories situated along the two mighty rivers that border the state of Missouri on its east and west. Also included are bluffs purely for viewing pleasure along the Katy Trail or bordering the idyllic, scenic streams and rivers of the Missouri Ozarks as well as in western Illinois and eastern Kansas.

Most of these bluffs are located on public lands and can be reached by well-worn paths or paved trails. A few of the bluffs described in this book are located on or near private property. The rights of landowners should always be respected, and some bluff adventures may require permits or special permission.

Unlike the rim of the Grand Canyon with its occasional signs warning that "People Die Here," few of the bluffs in the Midwest are posted with cautionary notices about the dangers of heights. Nevertheless, take heed. Bluff adventures can be lethal. Serious injuries and deaths have resulted from straying too close to bluff top edges or from amateur climbing up steep bluff walls.

If you are more in the market for an adrenaline rush, rather than simply having your breath taken away atop a tall bluff, then strongly consider joining a climbing club. Learn how to use the climber's belays, carabiners, cams, anchors, pitons and more. Learn the ropes—literally.

If this book inspires some readers to take up climbing, bouldering or rappelling, that's great. However, this work is tailored for those intent on tamer pursuits. Its purpose has to do with capturing special moments in nature rather than scaling heights or achieving acrobatic movements at higher elevations. Its primary mission has to do with relaxation, contemplation and appreciation of the animate and inanimate aspects of these elevated pieces of the planet.

In recent years, states in the Midwest have become more protective of their portions of the planet. This entails, in part, a new sensitivity toward the environmental heritage of high places within their borders.

Committed bluff lovers should be in the forefront of encouraging state conservation and natural resource departments to preserve these special places.

The integrity and viability of bluff lands can be lost because of poor environmental management; because of industry and quarry activities; because of developers who gobble up the best tracts for multimillion-dollar McMansion houses. Some bluff lands call out for crucial protections and should be declared part of our state and national public heritage.

The protective measures should not only cover the magnificent towers themselves, but also the hill prairies that often crown these nature sites. Hill prairies, cliffs and upper glades are home to unique herpetofauna—reptiles and amphibians. They also provide nesting for rare bird species that enjoy brisk bluff winds and the floodplains often situated below bluff spires.

Let us, however, put aside all the concern for these ledge-loving birds, narrowmouthed toads, coachwhip snakes and endangered high-cliff coneflowers. For heaven's sake, bluff habitat should be saved for human beings, too. We need the refuge of these ethereal places for our very sanity. They are locales for emotional and spiritual healing.

This book can be used as a guide to such locales and as a means to the refreshment of body and mind.

Let us, however, advise that no emotional or spiritual uplifting can take place if this book is misused. There are 30 bluff portraits contained in this book. The idea is not to rush from one corner of the state to the other to tally up bluff experiences. It is the curse of the western mind to turn everything into a race or a competition.

No one wins a prize if all 30 of these bluffs are taken in during a summer. And, in truth, there are far more than 30 bluffs contained in this seemingly small volume. For each bluff roost presents a dramatically different scene with spring, summer, fall and winter. That means there are actually 120 bluffs to behold in this book.

Consider a sitting each season on one of the many jutting exposures on the bluffs shown on the cover of this book—the south-facing cliffs at Castlewood Park. Each season brings different scenes; prompts different thoughts; raises different questions.

In summer, the eyes are drawn to the flow of the Meramec River below. A solitary canoeist appears out of the west, then begins to weave around the river's gravel bar beaches. Eighty years ago, these beaches were full of vacationers from the city. Where did they go? What happened?

In fall, the river is overwhelmed by fiery foliage—bright yellows and hot reds flutter from the trees. Their nuts and fruits drop to the cliff ledge then bounce off for an even longer descent. The trees know that it is time for their rest. How do we know when it is time for rest? Are we in touch with the natural rhythms of our own lives?

In winter, the rocky shelves of Castlewood are decorated with ice spears and frozen tinsel. Visit after a winter storm. The fields below will be asleep under blankets of snow, but not everything is in slumber. Animal tracks are everywhere. Which tracks were left by predators? Which tracks are of prey? On balance, is nature more mysterious or more cruel?

In spring, Castlewood's cliffs come alive with songbirds and come aglow in wildflowers. Who is happiest now? Is it the hawks circling overhead or the frogs singing in unison in the bottomlands below? Or, is it this temporary cliff dweller who feels a south wind upon the cheeks?

Of course, these bluffs not only transform with the changing seasons. They are dramatically different from dawn, to midday, to dusk. That means there are actually 360 bluffs contained in this book. Bluffs are nature's jesters. Their protean forms change with the circle of the seasons and the cycle of the days.

It should be conceded, finally, that the towering cliff nature sites in this book may not include all the best bluffs to be found in the heartland. Don't argue about it. Find your own bluffs! Create your own kind of bluff experiences! This book is simply a catalyst for cliff capers. It is the beginning of many journeys, surely not the trail's end. So, enjoy your "high country" explorations, enjoy some new horizons, and above all, be safe about it.

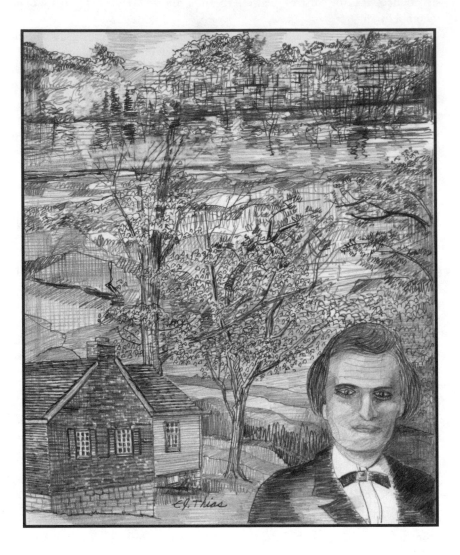

Bluff City of Arrow Rock

Long before there was a town, there was a bluff. Arrow Rock Bluff was favored as a valuable location by Native American tribes for centuries before settlers came upon it.

Native Americans visited the bluff area, situated along the west side of the Missouri River in the Booneslick region, for its nearby salt licks and for its accessible supply of hillside flint for making arrowheads.

Meriwether Lewis and William Clark noted that Arrow Rock would be a fine location for a town in their expedition journals. A quarter century after Lewis and Clark made their recommendation, a frontier town was founded on the bluff.

Even before it became the site for a bustling backwoods trading post, the bluff overlooked a ferry crossing for traders and travelers of the Santa Fe Trail. River traffic and the western trail helped the town grow in importance in 19th-century America.

When you come to see the Arrow Rock Bluff, you will, no doubt, be captivated by the town's history, landmarks and many ghosts of the past. Arrow Rock, today, has shrunk from its heyday to less than 100 souls.

Visitors will delight in seeing the Lyceum Theatre, Lodge Hall, Huston Tavern, Sappington Museum and the House of Bingham. George Caleb Bingham, who lived from 1811–1879, was known as "the Missouri Artist."

What better vantage point from which to be the Missouri Artist than the flinty bluff of Arrow Rock. From that high point, Bingham captured Missouri river life—the raftsmen, dugout travelers, canoeists, the flatboaters and steamboat crews.

From his fur traders to his jolly flatboatmen, Bingham created images that are full of bright colors and vitality. They are expressions of progress, optimism and expansion of a nation, both in its physicality and idealism.

Perhaps Bingham's best-known work, *Jolly Flatboatmen in Port,* is a grand portrait of American commerce and character. Boat hands on deck are in various stages of revelry, thanks to a happy fiddler and dancing boatman. Strike up a tune; we are in port.

Critics of Bingham say his work is naive, provincial and lacks depth. His boatmen are sweet children, rather than crude ruffians. His river is placid and inviting, rather than wild, wandering and dangerous.

Of course, today's wide Missouri has been channelized and denatured. The river traffic is but a trickle compared to Bingham's era. What's more, the river has shifted a mile away and is no longer within easy sight of the bluff where Bingham made his home.

Even so, the sight of Bingham's home and his backyard bluff at Arrow Rock are a wonder to behold. Imagine Missouri's Artist here putting together those happy river visions. Forget Bingham's critics and the naysayers. Listen to the boater's music, the hoots and the hollers in the distance.

BEE TREE PARK REFLECTIONS

LOTS OF FOLKS GIVE THOUGHT TO IDEAS OF GREAT ADVENTURE; FAR FEWER ACTUALLY TAKE THE RISKS TO TURN FANTASIES INTO REALITY. If you are mulling over a life change or an unusual quest, Bee Tree Park may be a useful place to contemplate the challenges you face.

The park, a few miles south of St. Louis, includes the Nims Mansion overlooking the Mississippi River. The stone mansion once housed the Golden Eagle River Museum, founded by the appreciative former passengers of the overnight steamboat.

The museum collection featured items like the original steam whistle, riverboat bells, tableware and other artifacts. Those have been moved to a new museum in Cape Girardeau, but there are rumors that the ghost of an old riverboat captain remains, haunting the stately river mansion.

Not far from the mansion is the half-mile Mississippi Trail, which takes you along the river bluff and to the Chubb Memorial Overlook. The gazebo-like, pavilion overlook is the perfect place to consider your hopes, your ambitions, your dreams.

The overlook provides a panoramic view of the Mississippi and the towboat traffic below. If you squint your eyes hard enough, and click your heels three times, you may just catch the ghost of Mark Twain at the wheel of the steamboat *Crescent City*, heading south for a trip to New Orleans.

In his *Life on the Mississippi*, Twain described all of his fleeting childhood ambitions, from circus performer to pirate. The ambition to be a steamboat pilot never faded.

The risks involved in river travel were many. Banks changed regularly; winds created dangerous reefs; and underwater snags frequently sent sturdy boats to river's bottom.

Twain came to know the risks of river adventure early, when boilers exploded on his poor brother Henry's steamship near Memphis. His lungs scalded by inhaled steam, Henry was blown out into the water and later died of his injuries in a Memphis hospital with Twain at his side.

Despite the tragedy and the ever-present risks, Twain continued carrying out his river dream until the Civil War broke out. Twain said his stint as a river pilot gave him enough schooling in human nature and character for a lifetime of story writing.

Twain put aside all of his fearful thoughts to fulfill an aspiration that later became an inspiration for his great literary achievement. His river adventure was but a tributary to a much larger body of accomplishment.

In a vigorous and full life, safe banks will disappear; winds will create perilous reefs; underwater snags will threaten the journey. What to do? Should you consider just staying put—treading safe water where you are?

Bee Tree's bluffs may be the place to consider future paths. Don't be surprised if the ghost of Mark Twain has a say in your deliberations.

Hoopla at Benedictine Bluffs

Benedictine College in Atchison, Kan., is built on a beautiful bluff line overlooking the last stretch of the Missouri River before it finds its way north to Nebraska. These bluff overlooks face east to Missouri and are of historic, as well as aesthetic, import.

My first introduction to the bluffs was marked by neither an appreciation of the historic, nor the visual rewards, of the region's heights. The bluffs have traditionally been a site for Benedictine college boys to fire up their spirits before the sports encounters of their Ravens' teams.

During my transient college years, I had the opportunity to visit the school—and the boys on the bluff—when this Catholic institution was still a bastion of male hubris. As God is my witness, I profess that nothing ever will compare to the pre-game festivities that occurred in the bluff area.

Spirits ran particularly high before Benedictine College contests with rival Rockhurst, whose Hawks hailed from Kansas City. Someone was bound to be bloodied when the talons of Hawks and Ravens were bared.

Is it an irony, a coincidence or some strange kind of synchronicity that this Benedictine river bluff area was recognized as a good party site long before the college was established?

In fact, the Lewis and Clark expedition stopped near the foot of the bluffs to celebrate the first 4th of July west of the Mississippi in 1804. The explorers fired their swivel canon twice and everyone got an extra gill from the whiskey barrel.

Some days before arriving at the Benedictine site, two members of the expedition were punished for getting into the whiskey, an incident near today's Kansas City. Perhaps Lewis and Clark took this indiscretion as a sign the crew needed a break and a place for a little downtime to raise spirits. How appropriate that the Benedictine site filled the bill on July 4, 1804.

Today, the college actually has outfitted two sites for looking out over the Missouri River and what was the Lewis and Clark encampment. Abbey Lookout Point is situated next to the stolid five-story St. Benedict's Abbey. Monks quarried the limestone for the abbey building from below the bluffs.

Abbey Lookout provides an awesome view of the "Great Bend of the Missouri River." A second promontory, Ravenswood Overlook, offers a view of the river valley more than four miles across. You can also see remnants of a trail heading down from the overlook.

The trail has existed since the earliest Americans settled the area. It may have even originated with Native Americans seeking higher ground from the river basin below.

For breathtaking river vistas and also to view "one of the most butifull Plains I ever Saw," according to Meriwether Lewis, consider a visit to Benedictine College. You might even schedule your trip to take in a rowdy game of Ravens versus Hawks.

CARDAREVA: CHOCTAW CHIEF'S BLUFF

As a youth who came of age on the flats of the Land of Lincoln, I jumped at any chance to travel the hills and rivers of Ozarkia—to "Injun" territory and the hideouts of Jesse James.

Alas, my parents were not inclined to such travel adventures. Fortunately, my since-departed Uncle Stanley did love to pack up a car full of kids and head to the bluffs and springs of the Mark Twain National Forest. And I readily accepted all invitations to come along.

Nature-loving, outdoor-types like good old Uncle Stanley should come standard in the lives of youngsters, particularly those confined to growing up in urbs and suburbs.

As we exited from civilization's outer limits, Uncle Stanley would be driving and leading a chorus of kids in "100 Bottles of Beer on the Wall." By the time we turned onto a highway south to meet up with Current River country, we were well into "Green grow, the lilacs grow."

Uncle Stanley knew all the must-see spots along the riverway: Akers Ferry, Round Spring, Owls Bend, Big Spring. When we kids grew older, the sight-seeing trips evolved into canoe float expeditions. We marveled at the bluffs between places named Pulltite, Jerktail Landing and Log Yard; and we wondered whether Injuns were aiming arrows at us from the bluffs.

Eventually, we outgrew trips with Uncle Stanley. We became college kids planning our own Current River trips with canoes overloaded with food and drink. Our loud laughter and riotous yelling would echo off the canyon walls and into the Current's valleys.

Oblivious to all perils or the beauty surrounding us, we carried on to such an extent that we failed to see "sweepers" hanging across the river. These were large, low-hanging tree limbs that knocked us from our vessels, dumped our canoes and scattered our precious provisions far down river.

Now, we wiser veterans of Uncle Stanley's Ozark tours have entered a new stage in life. When we paddle the waters of the Current, we give our due to nature. We ask forgiveness of the hills, bluffs and springs for our past slights and the gross impertinence we displayed on youthful voyages.

Certainly Cardareva Bluff, midway between Blue Spring and Paint Rock Bluff, merits a certain awe and homage from all water-borne passers-by. This craggy bluff calls for adoration, especially in October, when it reveals more of itself, even as it is dressed in the many fine colors of fall's foliage.

Named for a Choctaw chief who once led his tribe in this lush area of Ozark flora and fauna, Cardareva is a monument when viewed from below and a prime lookout when scaled and gloried from above.

Chief Cardareva is buried near the summit of the mountain that bears his name. So, let us offer this petition: "Oh, Great Chief, we troops of Uncle Stanley acknowledge your presence—the magnificence of Cardareva."

CASTLEWOOD'S RIVER SCENE TRAIL

REGULARS AT CASTLEWOOD STATE PARK CONTEND THAT THE MERAMEC BLUFFS AT THE PARK ARE THE BEST HIGH PLACES TO BE FOUND IN THE ENTIRE ST. LOUIS REGION. Watch a red summer sunset on the bluffs, or witness the Meramec valley in a white blanket after a blustery winter night's storm, and you'll be hard-pressed to argue with partisans of Castlewood's Meramec bluffs.

Some folks who enter the park on Kiefer Creek Road will immediately drive to the trailhead at River Scene. That first trailhead takes you immediately up to the bluffs' incredible vistas. However, there are rewards to be found in a little delayed gratification.

Consider starting your bluff hike at the second trailhead, which can be found on the right after driving under a railroad tunnel. Hike west below the bluffs. You'll be between the Meramec River and those very active railroad tracks that hug the base of the bluffs. It's a pretty walk. About a mile down, you'll find another tunnel under the tracks to a path that takes you up to the park's "Stairway to Heaven."

As you climb the series of wooden staircases—and stop on its platforms to catch your breath—you will spot the broken concrete foundations of old club houses, cabins and stores. These are the ruins of the park's resort era, when as many as 10,000 city dwellers would come by train, trolley and boat to enjoy summer weekends.

From the top of the staircase and along the bluffs to the east, you can see the Meramec sandbars and vestiges of Lincoln Beach, where swimmers and watercraft choked the river up until the 1950s.

Old timers in the area enjoy telling tales of illegal whiskey and gambling at Castlewood resort in its heyday during Prohibition. After a hot day of swimming, canoeing and card-playing along the beaches, the party crowd would dance on river decks. Still later, they would retire to cabins and hotels to enjoy home brew and illegal hooch.

Castlewood's hills and hollers were alive with the sound of music and partying into the wee hours of morning. According to local old timers, St. Louis County law enforcement not only looked the other way, but warned all those who owned slot machines and who "pitched whiskey" about any raids in the making by the Feds.

The arrival of interstate highways and plush Lake of the Ozarks resorts spelled the death knell for Castlewood as a weekend destination. Cabins, hotels and bathhouses fell into disrepair and were torn down. Meramec River floods also played a role in ripping away the past and carrying it downstream to oblivion.

It's inspiring to realize how nature has, at least at Castlewood, reclaimed a bit of its own. Look down from the bluffs, and you see that the beaches are not packed with the party crowd of the past. Instead, hawks circle the bottomland and blue heron can be seen foraging along the river banks. So be it.

Frenchman's Bluff Reflections

Peaks, pinnacles and bluffs have always been sought out as places to seek spiritual comfort—to implore the skies above and the ether beyond to answer heartfelt entreaties and the eternal questions.

The impulse seems universal, as religious tracts from any number of faiths chronicle their prophets and holy men trekking up the mountainside to seek guidance from above.

Moses sought wisdom from on high and was provided commandments to guide the future of mankind. Jesus sought inspiration on a sacred mount, and was soon delivering one of the greatest sermons in human history.

Today, New Age faith seekers stake out higher ground for rejuvenation, heavenly visions and unique insights. New Age therapists sometimes speak of geophysical frequencies and magnetic resonances as explanations for the special effects of high places.

While Missouri may not have a Mount Shasta, or the towers of the Rocky Mountains or Appalachians, the state does have its own modest peaks. River bluffs, pinnacle formations and Ozark outcroppings abound.

In other words, there are higher places here to seek sustenance for the spirit. One of the lesser-known limestone blufflines, situated between St. Charles and Hannibal, can be found in the 6,200-acre Cuivre River State Park.

The park includes a towering rock wall of Mississippi limestone, which affords visitors a sweeping view of the horizon. An ample supply of overlook sites are available for communing with nature, the universe, and most certainly, the eternal.

The best sites are to be found on Frenchman's Bluff. The name recalls the area's first white visitors, Louis Joliet and Pere Marquette, and the many French missionaries who followed with their stories and parables of a religion from the Old World.

As an occasional bluff dweller, this writer likes to consult their account of the temptation of Jesus. After 40 days and nights of fasting, Jesus was on a pinnacle of the temple, where Satan dared him: "If thou be the son of God, cast thyself down!"

Satan suggested Jesus could show himself as God for all to see, because the angels by "their hands shall bear thee up." Satan's ploy may have been a tempting way for Jesus to show his divinity, but it was a scheme to foil the true purpose of his time on earth.

Although this is a biblical story, it also is a parable for those who come to high places in search of easy spiritual fixes. Resist the temptation. If you go to the bluffs to meditate on desires you want fulfilled, save yourself the hike. If you scale the heights in quest of some benevolent genie who lives in a lamp, spare yourself the dare.

The rewards of reflecting on a high bluff are more experiential and relational than they are tangible. Don't be lured by high expectations, and by all means, don't "cast thyself down."

CURSING BLUFFS AT DEVIL'S ELBOW

MISSOURIANS ARE FOND OF REFERRING TO THEIR OUTSTATE WONDERLAND AS "GOD'S COUNTRY." How strange then that so many natural wonders of the back country are associated with Old Beelzebub himself—Satan.

For example, a rugged area with deep hollows and tall bluffs, southwest of Willow Springs, is known as the Devil's Backbone Wilderness. The spine of Satan resurfaces at several other locations in Missouri, including a ridge with great views near the Current River and Gladden Creek, known as the Devil's Backbone.

Greene County in the state's sinkhole and cave region boasts a small, but captivating, collapsed cavern dubbed by locals as the Devil's Den.

In the Ozark's Ha Ha Tonka Spring region and beyond, there are numerous limestone and dolomite structures with names such as Devil's Kitchen and Devil's Promenade.

A popular summertime haunt at Rock Bridge Memorial State Park in Columbia is Devil's Ice Box, a deep chasm and cavern opening that offers a bit of nature's air-conditioning when Missouri temperatures soar.

Of course, Taum Sauk Mountain has its infamous Devil's Tollgate, a very narrow, rocky passage which the Cherokee squeezed through on their forced resettlement from the southeast to less verdant lands.

If you decide to take a trek through "God's Country" to visit all the sites staked out for the devil, you should certainly include the Devil's Elbow, which can be found south of Rolla and I-44 on the Big Piney River.

Devil's Elbow Bluffs are claimed as among the most beautiful in the state by seasoned canoeists. Paddlers who are new to the area will find the bluffs between Shanghai Spring and the Big Piney's junction with the Gasconade River to the north.

It's possible to reach the bluffs on foot, but this requires some hiking on private land. Rock climbers have been known to traverse the cracks, faces and cliffs of Devil's Elbow after seeking permission from landowners.

If you are wondering how in the devil this area and the bluffs gained the name of the Prince of Darkness, residents will tell you that it goes back to the region's logging days. The hamlet of Devil's Elbow itself is named for the sharp river bend which was a hazard for log rafters.

Lumberjacks cursed the log jams at the bend that put the rafters in harm's way, while holding up their commerce in wood. That kind of chaos disappeared from this river a century ago, though canoeists still complain about having to wade past obstacles hung up in this stretch of the river.

If you go to Devil's Elbow, be sure to check out the huge semi-cylinder bluff with the rock "lid" known as the Devil's Sugar Bowl. But, please, show no sympathy for the Devil. Instead, say a prayer for the long-departed lumberjacks of Devil's Elbow.

Easley: Try to Catch the Wind

Have you ever tried to catch the wind? Throughout the ages, the wind has been a favorite subject of poets and lyricists. It is mysterious and elusive, yet we know it is there. But can you ever actually catch it?

Just as a successful fishing trip requires knowing where to catch the big ones, any serious attempt to catch the wind requires knowing where the air is most accessible—where it is in most abundance.

Bluffs of the Missouri River Valley provide excellent vantage points for catching the wind. My favorite bluffs are within a 70-mile radius of Jefferson City, a river city capital. Of course, Jefferson City has its own voluminous wind when its statehouse is in session. But that's not what we are talking about here.

Moving downstream from the state capital, you can find the bluffs of wine country: Mokane and Rhineland, Hermann and Augusta. Moving upstream from Jeff City, the river turns northwest, where you can find the bluffs of Easley and Rocheport.

Rocheport's lovely heights are well known. Easley's bluffs are less familiar because they are more isolated, though that is changing with the growing popularity of the Katy Trail that runs beneath them.

My rural roommates introduced me to Easley, when I was a grad student at the University of Missouri. They took me to Easley to shoot their handguns. We would climb the bluffs to a small cave that they favored.

I had no use for firearms. So, while they sent rusty tin cans to a harsh demise, I sat on the bluffs and enjoyed the brisk winds upon my face. In spring, moist winds from the Gulf and northerlies from Canada fight for dominance. Westerlies bring angry weather to settle these disputes.

On an April afternoon, I recall stiff winds from the south raising the temperatures to summer levels, kicking up waves on the river below. Weather reports spoke of tornadic storms coming in from the Great West. A thousand miles away, north winds were burying the foothills west of Colorado Springs, Denver and Boulder in snow.

Missouri's river bluffs are great places to feel the energy of seasons changing. On these cliffs, you can witness the last gasps of winter, or perhaps a summer trying desperately to stave off the inevitable fall. They are noble battles, but in the end, the appointed seasons must prevail.

It is natural to sometimes lament the ever-turning wheel of the seasons and of life. Nature shows us the way to face and to embrace these winds of change, rather than to run away.

Have you ever tried to catch the wind?

Of course, you have. When life's travails seem to sap all of your energy, even your will—you are winded. You must try to catch your breath. Sit a spell on Easley's bluffs, and you just might catch a second wind.

Fults Prairie Hill Bluff

Jutting bluffs of Fults Hill Nature Preserve in southern Illinois provide spectacular vistas of the Mississippi River Valley. Located along Bluff Road, south of Vallmeyer, Ill., these rocky cliffs ascend from a usually marshy area known as Kidd Lake.

From the Fults Bluffs, you can see for miles up and down the river bottoms. Large hawks, turkey vultures and eagles may soar close to you at these heights, as they enjoy the same views that have inspired you to make the climb to their level.

Directly below, you will see ducks, geese, herons and many other inhabitants of the marsh. Muskrats thrive here and you will, no doubt, see their dome structures dotting the soggy river bottomland.

Farther out, you will find a patchwork of beautiful, fertile farmland that dissolves into rows of trees that stand as sentries along the river, which can expand to great widths in this region. Across the Mississippi are the wooded hills that are home to many small villages of Missouri.

The overlooks of Fults offer scenery to die and go to heaven for. However, if you find the lovely views "breath-taking," you're probably missing out on the real life-giving potential here that can sometimes overwhelm visitors to this site.

For the bluffs of Fults should be a place to catch your breath, not to lose it. These rocky ledges should be a place to slow down your breathing—to quiet the chatter in your life—and to meditate on the beauty of green earth below and blue sky above.

One of my first visits to the Fults Bluffs was when I was in graduate school. A friend brought a transistor radio along to catch a Cards baseball game. The game was interrupted by a bulletin about the resignation of Spiro T. Agnew and the deepening crisis of President Nixon's Watergate. It was a time of world turmoil, fall of 1973.

As I sat in thick, deep prairie grass on Fults Bluffs, I listened to the stories of torment in the Middle East and of tumult in Washington, D.C. I felt so fortunate to be "one of the little people," on these bluffs, far away from the chaos of cities and nations. It was time to turn the radio off and enjoy the here and now of nature's way.

One of the natural aspects that makes Fults so unique is that this area is prairie. It's prairie on a hill—not on a plain! Near and above the rock shelf overlooks are prairie grasses, wildflowers and sumac that shows bright red as winter approaches.

A natural mecca, Fults should inspire a pilgrimage all four seasons. Seasonal changes can be marvelous. Fall and spring are extra spectacular.

The best way to enjoy Fults is to make a nest for yourself in the thick prairie grass. Make sure it's a nest with a view. If you are a neophyte at meditation, simply look out from your nest and focus on your breathing.

Fults is the perfect location to exhale the poisons of emotional and mental stress, while at the same time inhaling the air, light and energy of a hillside prairie paradise.

The View from Green's Cave Bluff

In the classic movie, *Deliverance,* based on the novel by James Dickey, mountain men spy from atop a bluff on unsuspecting city folk trying to negotiate the wily river below.

You can get a sense of the good old boys' perspective—from their lofty, secret vantage point—by taking a summer hike on Bluff View Trail at Meramec State Park. The state park, located southeast of Sullivan, offers a variety of trails with river overlooks.

Bluff View Trail provides views of river activity from several ledges that are camouflaged with thick foliage. The summer scenes below are not always inspiring. They often consist of flailing arms and floating alabaster torsos roasting to a fiery red, hours before the sun sets on the horizon.

Oh, to have lived in an earlier era of authentic Meramec River human habitation—those old days when river folk included old Ralph "Treehouse" Brown, "Squirrel Baggin'" Joe Schele, and Emma Crow, otherwise known by her accomplices as "The Squaw."

All these legendary river characters are described in the heavily illustrated *Canoeing God's Gifts,* by Al, Syl and Frank Beletz. The Beletz brothers formed the now-defunct Meramec Canoe Club, which thrived as early as the 1930s and as late as the 1970s.

Of course, the river gang chronicled by the Beletz boys would not have been content to splash around in the tame area of Bluff View Trail. It's a better bet that they would be found in far more dramatic environs upriver around Green's Cave Bluff.

The bluff and cave are depicted in a wonderful mural at Meramec State Park's visitors center. If you are not up for a long, rugged hike upriver from the state park, you may be content with the mural. However, if you want the real thing, Green's Cave Bluff is accessible by foot or by canoe.

It's about a two-mile canoe trip from the park to the site. The cave is a wonder by itself; the bluff is icing on the cake. A trail up to the bluff takes you up 140 feet above the river with great views of the Meramec below.

Imagine the sights of yesteryear from these heights: Joe Schele passing by with a canoe full of squirrels destined for a stew on a late-night campfire; hunky Ralph Brown poling upstream to the Huzzah to his treehouse home; Emma Crow with caged chickens in her craft for a later campsite meal of freshly butchered bird.

The Beletz brothers of St. Louis canoed the Meramec with these rakes and rogues. They loved the river rats, the river lore, and the great river landmarks—such as Green's Cave Bluff. They also joined in the 1970s' fight to save the Meramec from being dammed for a giant motorboat lake.

Some say the cave and the bluff's beauty would have been lost to a new dam and lake. The Beletz boys are skeptics. Because of caverns, caves and sinkholes in the area, they think the project would not have held water.

Bluffs Above Laughing Waters

When selecting a cover photo to mark the 75th birthday of Missouri state parks in 1992, it's no surprise the Department of Natural Resources chose Ha Ha Tonka for its quarterly magazine's anniversary issue.

The *Resource Review* cover shows stone ruins of the Scottish-style castle at Ha Ha Tonka, situated high atop the bluff wall overlooking the Niangua Arm of the Lake of the Ozarks. The castle walls mirror those solid bluffs and, in fact, the stone that made those fortress walls was quarried from nearby rock veins.

Of course, it's the water that made Ha Ha Tonka famous. Ha Ha Tonka Spring once sent water—50 million gallons of it every day—crashing over a rock and gravel bed on its way to the Niangua River. The sound of that enormous cascade is said to have inspired resident Native Americans to name it Ha Ha Tonka, the place of "Laughing Water."

The great laugh was reduced to less than a giggle in the early 1930s when Bagnell Dam made dragon-like fingers to create Lake of the Ozarks. One of the great fingers was actually an arm, the Niangua Arm, and it submerged Ha Ha Tonka beneath a pool.

If you want to hear the laughing of Ha Ha Tonka now, you'd best have some diving equipment. Long before the laughing water fell silent, legend has it that northern tribes of Native Americans wintered by the great spring of water that wouldn't freeze.

A lot more lore could be written about "Laughing Water," its history and its fate, but it's all water under the bridge—or a pool—at this point. It's time now to turn your attention to those marvelous, 250-foot bluffs.

If you're a bluff lover, no doubt you've climbed to heights you never want to leave and dreamt of having a home at the apex. Imagine the view from your picture window of mighty bluffs descending below, thick stands of pines in the distance and an ice-covered lake—all covered in a dusting of powdered-sugar snow glistening under a winter sun.

A rich Kansas City businessman named Snyder was not content to just dream when he found Ha Ha Tonka's heights. After a visit to the area in the early 1900s, he bought the land and began building his dream home. His home truly was to be his castle, but he died before its completion in a car crash.

The castle was completed by his son in 1922, but it was gutted two decades later after sparks from a fireplace set the wooden roof on fire. After years of neglect, the land and shell of the 60-room mansion was sold to the Nature Conservancy and subsequently acquired by the state for the park.

So many Ha Ha Tonka stories can fire the imagination when traversing the 70 acres of this park. A trail called Castle Bluff will get you up to the ruins. Ha Ha Tonka is a wonder of a park, but it's hard not to grow a little melancholy at the thought of the loss of the castle and the water's laughter.

HANNIBAL'S LOVER'S LEAP

ARE YOU FEELING LOW? Then seek out higher ground. Higher places—cliffs, hilltops and bluffs—have always been sought out by those seeking a sacred experience or some heavenly deliverance from cruel reality.

In the Hannibal of the boy Sam Clemens, who would later be known as Mark Twain, two hilltops were within walking distance for villagers seeking higher ground. These hilltops along the Mississippi continue to frame the sleepy little river town.

On the north is Cardiff Hill, topped with a historic lighthouse; on the south is Lover's Leap, adorned with a plaque detailing the native myth behind the mound's monicker. The myth concerns a brash and daring Pawnee warrior in love with a young Indian woman of the Missouri Fox Tribe. When the Fox chief finds out about their secret relationship, he ambushes the two lovers as they rendezvous on the towering bluff.

At the sight of the Fox chief stretching his bow to aim an arrow at his own daughter, the Pawnee grabs his lover's arm and jumps off the bluff—tumbling over together into the ether of mythology.

The local legend of the Pawnee warrior and the Fox princess may please tourists and meet the needs of the Convention and Visitors Bureau of today's Hannibal. However, it may not be the best story associated with the high bluff on Hannibal's southern edge.

Consider, instead, one of Twain's recollections. On his last visit to Hannibal before his death, Twain recalled how the religious sect, the Millerites, put on their robes one evening and hiked up the bluff.

The Millerites believed that God would hear their entreaties and deliver them to heaven from the high perch of Lover's Leap. None of them ascended that night. They were, no doubt, embarrassed by the morning sunrise. Twain recalled that the town shared in their embarrassment.

Of course, plenty of religious folks are convinced today that God will be taking them physically up to heaven. They include millennialists, anticipaters of Armaggedon, and those packed and ready for Rapture.

While it may be tempting for skeptics to laugh at the hopes of the faithful, there is little mirth in considering the motivation of those seeking deliverance from the travails of this world. A hike up and a walk around Hannibal's Lover's Leap offers at least a temporary respite from worldly strife and trauma.

When visiting Lover's Leap, look to the north and imagine Mark Twain as a boy frolicking in the town below. Look straight ahead to the river that carried him off to a mad adult world full of triumph and loss. Then reflect on how Twain confronted all adversity with a sobering wit: "All say, 'How hard it is that we have to die'—a strange complaint to come from the mouths of people who have had to live."

Shady Bluffs Border Pickle Creek

Reaching the summit of a line of bluffs on a scorching Midwest summer day can be a mixed blessing. Sure, the views are great; but the heat can be downright intolerable.

Besides the heat, consider your company on the cliffs—cacti and occasionally even a scorpion. Nearby brush can be a home for pesky chiggers and ticks, ready for any opportunity to relocate—on you.

For this reason, many backpackers and hikers prefer late fall or early spring for adventures. The hardiest of the lot actually prefer winter at its coldest. They'll talk of cliffs hung with icicles; waterfalls frozen into crystalline sculptures. They'll swoon over bare trees and unobstructed vistas.

It's a worthy sport—debating which season presents nature at its finest. In truth, you can be a happy explorer for all seasons. Shun weather extremes. Weigh all the outdoor variables when deciding where to go.

When summer throws its worst at you, it's hard to find a better destination than Hawn State Park, in part, because of its shaded trails and bluffs. Hawn State Park, located in southeast Missouri west of Ste. Genevieve, is a best bet for a summer expedition.

This contention is based on my own mid-summer's family safari, when mutiny seemed a virtual certainty. With a heat index in the triple digits, it was a feat just to pry sweltering humans from a car at the trailhead.

However, once in the woods, the grumbling abated. Tall, majestic pines kept the harsh sun at bay. Mom found the sound of the nearby stream far more soothing than kids in a car. A son cooled his feet by wading in Pickle Creek. A daughter sprawled out on a rock bluff looking down on the creek.

And the best thing about that bluff was that it was sheltered. A canopy of leafy trees almost kept you guessing whether the day was still sunny or now overcast. A cooling breeze came by to inspire the leaves into a low chorus to accompany the gurgling waters meandering down Pickle Creek.

Hawn State Park boasts miles of looping trails. It's a backpacker's paradise. Several backpack campsites are provided for overnighters. However, if you're saddled with a family that is tentative in its enthusiasm for nature hiking—don't push it. Take the short, but rewarding, two-mile loop combination of Pickle Creek Trail and Whispering Pine Trail.

Nature hiking doesn't have to be an endurance sport or a long-distance marathon. Take time, as they say, to smell the flowers; to splash around in the creek; to close your eyes and unfurl your tired body on top of a smooth, bare-rock, table-top bluff.

Who knows what you will take away from the experience. Perhaps a portrait of a bluff and your daughter, suitable for framing. Perhaps a little peace of mind—knowing you've found a ready refuge from the harshest elements of our existence.

HUGHES MOUNTAIN MARVEL

VISTAS FROM HUGHES MOUNTAIN ARE AWESOME ENOUGH, BUT IT'S THE SUMMIT ITSELF THAT WILL AMAZE YOU. Located between Caledonia and Irondale in Washington County, it's a short hike to get to the amazing top of Hughes.

The summit is a marvel of chimney-like rock formations from the pre-Cambrian period—more than a billion years ago. A single trail up to, and through, the high plateau of Hughes is called Devil's Honeycomb Trail.

Initial trailblazers called it Devil's Honeycomb because of its odd, tightly packed aggregations of small rock columns. They jut and sprawl from the hillsides all across the site.

Hughes Mountain could just as easily be called the home of the Mad Stonemason. The place looks like it was inhabited by a very strange stonemason who started one foundation only to move to another and another—never finishing a job.

All that craggy rhyolite rock can take a toll on your feet. Fortunately, the formations are broken up by smooth, buried boulders covered with lichens. On a hot summer's day, your feet will appreciate walking the soft lichen carpets, after negotiating the patchwork of jagged rhyolite.

One of the interesting aspects of Hughes is what hikers invariably leave behind after their visits. Loose stone bricks and blocks, high atop Hughes, apparently inspire the architect, the builder, the visionary locked up within visiting hikers.

At Hughes Mountain, you might stumble upon flat rocks stacked up like scale model skyscrapers, or like sacrificial altars or shrines or pagodas. You may find that someone has arranged a circle of stones resembling the ancient ritual monument of Stonehenge near Salisbury, England.

Hughes Mountain may actually be a more intriguing destination than Stonehenge at this point in our time. After all, tourist buses now crowd the ancient site in England, and visitors are cordoned off from getting too close to its upright stones. Concerns over security at Stonehenge have necessitated that visits are a completely passive experience.

Not so with Hughes Mountain. Here you can amble among the billion-year-old rhyolite and pick up the loose stones to create your own modest tombs, totems or temples.

Perhaps you'll be inspired to emulate the builders of Stonehenge by erecting rock markers that coincide with important celestial positions of the sun and moon.

Then again, you may just want to send any pillars of stone—erected and left by previous visitors—crashing to the ground. You may just want Hughes Mountain to appear natural, untouched by human invention.

Should you yield to a temptation to send past hikers' monuments tumbling at Hughes Mountain, don't feel too guilty. Consider that the Romans tore down and desecrated much of Stonehenge, long before the tour buses arrived.

PLEASURES OF LES BOURGEOIS BLUFFS

THE ENJOYMENT OF TALL BLUFF SUMMITS DOESN'T ALWAYS HAVE TO COME WITH A HEAVY PRICE, SUCH AS THE SWEAT EQUITY OF A LONG HIKE OR THE NERVE-WRACKING ANXIETY OF A PRECARIOUS CLIMB.

Sometimes the price of admission is no more than, say, a bottle of sweet Missouri vineyard wine. That is certainly the case when it comes to the Les Bourgeois Bluffs which overlook the Missouri River and the Katy Trail area of nearby Rocheport.

The view from these bluffs is just a short walk from the Les Bourgeois Vineyards' parking lot. The lot is a few minutes north of I-70, once you get off the interstate at the exit for Rocheport. And the exit to Rocheport is just east of the interstate bridge over the Missouri River.

Les Bourgeois offers two sites from which to experience the bluffs. The more formal location is the Blufftop Bistro. I have yet to be disappointed with the food or views at this spectacular, timber-frame restaurant. It is a thrill to eat and imbibe, while experiencing shadows cast from hawks and eagles flying over the bistro skylights.

For more rustic encounters in the great outdoors, you may be drawn to the A-frame wine-tasting center, which anchors a series of multi-level decks looking out from Les Bourgeois Bluffs over the Missouri River.

My preference is for deck-sitting at the A-frame with a chilled bottle of Riverboat Red and whatever other companionship is available. This is my choice, except during a few short months when daylight is slight and sun no longer sufficiently warms.

On hot summer days, the terraced decks at Les Bourgeois can still be pleasant because of cooling valley breezes. My favorite river scenes are when weekend canoeists take guided trips on the Missouri River below. It's hard not to feel a bit smug, watching the river gang paddle their canoes, while sipping a cool glass of vino high above the thrashing and splashing.

Two hundred years ago, Lewis and Clark were the ones thrashing and splashing below. When their pioneer entourage stopped in this area, they were impressed by the scenery but put off by the abundance of bluff-dwelling rattle snakes. They quickly moved on to Arrow Rock and beyond.

Perhaps Lewis and Clark would have stayed longer had Les Bourgeois Vineyards been open. They would have certainly found it hard to resist writing in their journals about the sunsets from the Les Bourgeois Bluffs, or the full moons glimmering off the Missouri River waters at night.

In fairness, there are a number of other Show Me State vineyards along the Missouri River, where fine wines flow and bluff views abound. This is especially true of the Augusta and Hermann areas in eastern Missouri.

While all of these wonderful sites merit visits, a case can easily be made that Les Bourgeois Bluffs face best for sunsets and splendid river scenes.

BLUFFS OF LEWIS AND CLARK TRAILS

THE BLUFFS OF THE LEWIS AND CLARK TRAILS, LOCATED IN THE WELDON SPRING WILDLIFE AREA NEAR DEFIANCE, PROVIDE EXCELLENT SITES FOR CONTEMPLATING THE TRIUMPH AS WELL AS THE POTENTIAL FOLLY OF HUMANKIND.

The bluffs offer spectacular views, both north and south, of the Missouri River. This is where Meriwether Lewis and William Clark could be found in May 1804, at an early stage in their long triumphant journey to explore the great Northwest.

Lewis and Clark had an awe of the power of the river and equal respect for unpredictable nature. That respect was evident in the vast preparations the two made for their trip, described in Stephen E. Ambrose's *Lewis & Clark: Voyage of Discovery.*

Early on in their trip, the explorers were amazed at the snags, shifting sandbars, whirlpools and encroaching bluffs they found on the river. Captain Lewis, on a lookout detail, narrowly escaped injury in a fall from the bluffs in the Weldon Spring Wildlife area.

When you visit the bluff area, river history will come to life as you imagine the explorers' small flotilla heading upriver. The keelboats, dugouts and rowboats full of white men must have been a strange sight for Sioux, Shoshone, Mandan and other tribes that came upon the expedition.

The mission outlined by President Thomas Jefferson to Lewis and Clark for their travels remains instructive today. Jefferson was keenly interested in the habitat, plants and animals the two would find along the way, and asked that they take detailed notes.

Jefferson also asked that they take pains not to offend native peoples. He advised that belligerence be the last option in any misunderstandings. Lewis and Clark succeeded in carrying out Jefferson's directives, proving to be both diplomats and chroniclers of a new environment.

Of course, the river and the land covered by Lewis and Clark are quite different today. Look east from the trail bluffs, and you'll find massive floodplain development. More than $2 billion of commercial sprawl now covers the adjacent Chesterfield Valley across the river. In the Flood of 1993, this area was under tons of muddy Missouri River water. Developers came back to tempt fate by building new strip malls, franchise eateries and auto dealers.

The Monarch Levee, which gave way to the rampaging Missouri in 1993, had once been judged as a 100-year levee. A new, wider and higher levee is now regarded as a being capable of withstanding a 500-year flood.

Some engineers and environmentalists say it's folly to suggest the new levy will offer five centuries of protection—the river is too fickle and our altered nature is too unpredictable.

Looking back to the past from the trail bluffs, it is easy to see triumph in the Lewis and Clark mission. Looking ahead from these bluffs, ask yourself how the future will judge our present.

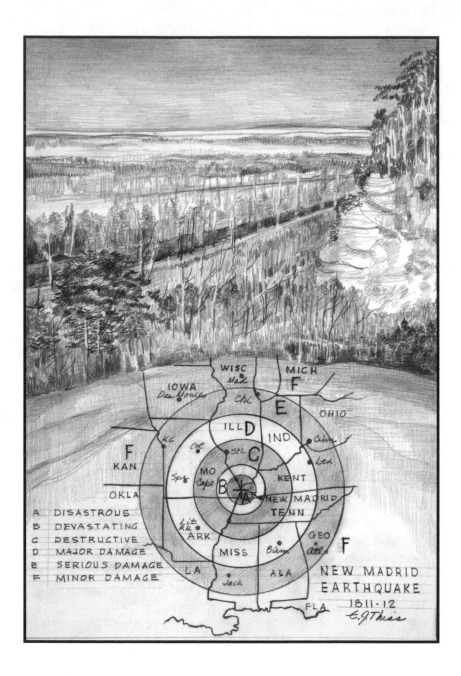

WISC Mad.
MICH
F
IOWA
Des Moines
Chi
E
OHIO
ILL
D
IND
Cinn
KC
Col
StL
Lex
F
KAN
Spr
MO
Cape
C
KENT
OKLA
B
A
NEW MADRID
TENN
Lit Rk
Ark
GEO
Atl
F
MISS
Birm
LA
Jack
ALA
NEW MADRID
EARTHQUAKE
FLA
1811-12
E.J.Theis

A   DISASTROUS
B   DEVASTATING
C   DESTRUCTIVE
D   MAJOR DAMAGE
E   SERIOUS DAMAGE
F   MINOR DAMAGE

LITTLE GRAND CANYON WANDERINGS

WHEN THE MISSISSIPPI VALLEY FAILED TO SHAKE, RATTLE OR ROLL AFTER IBEN BROWNING'S PREDICTION FOR A GREAT EARTHQUAKE IN DECEMBER 1990, SOME FOLKS DISMISSED HIM AS A QUACK.

Experts, however, suggest it's only a matter of time before there is a repeat of the disastrous New Madrid Earthquake of 1811–12. When it does occur, might the Mississippi shift east to again claim more of Illinois for the state of Missouri?

Will the great river once again flow backward? Will animals panic in the hours before the big quake hits? Will fantastic geysers of mud, sand and carbonized wood erupt from the wetlands and lowlands of river valleys?

Those kind of questions flood my shallow mind when contemplating a broad expanse of Mississippi River Valley from the bluffs at Little Grand Canyon. The canyon is located in the Shawnee National Forest of southern Illinois along the Big Muddy River.

The canyon bluffs rise above the bottomland more than 300 feet, and a creek that helped carve the heights into a canyon drops several hundred feet on its way to the Big Muddy. A circuitous hiking trail runs up along chalky bluffs, to a Mississippi Valley overlook, then to the canyon overlook.

Many bluff trails are little more than woodland hikes—they make up the hard work required to get to the reward of beautiful vistas. At Little Grand Canyon, the trail is a big part of the reward for your visit. The trail passes by sandstone walls, cascades, grottos and through dense forest.

Visual rewards from Little Grand Canyon heights include the sculpted cliffs at the canyon overlook on the east side of the trail loop, and the Mississippi Valley at its western edge. At that point, you can see Missouri's hills seven miles or more to the west.

Little Grand Canyon may invite comparisons to the real thing in northern Arizona. Do these Illinois bluffs constitute an east rim? Do those hills in Missouri make up the west rim? Is it fair to compare this nature site to the north rim or south rim of the Grand Canyon? No.

Nevertheless, any attempt to make comparisons prompts a few observations. When taking small fry to the actual Grand Canyon, it's hard not to be struck by the stern warning signs: "People Die Here." When hiking with little ones in any bluff area, keep in mind that a child can be just as dead from a 50-foot fall as from a half-mile Grand Canyon fall. Exercise care!

Another observation for all those worldly travelers who might belittle the Little Grand Canyon: Keep in mind that the real thing was formed by a half-billion years or more of Colorado River erosion, relentless carving winds and geological uplifts.

The Little Grand Canyon is quite young—a masterpiece still in the making. Who knows what this place will look like after a few more eons of action by the New Madrid Fault.

Park Campus Promontory

Parkville is a river town just north of Kansas City on a curly stretch of the Missouri River. A few miles to the south of it is Quindaro Bend. A few miles to the west is Pomeroy Bend.

Farther up the river from Parkville is the better-known Weston Bend on a twisting segment of the Big Muddy across from Fort Leavenworth in Kansas. With all these bends in the river, it should come as no surprise that many a steamboat took early retirement in this area of Missouri.

Of course, harrowing bends were in far more abundance in the 1800s, long before the river was channelized. The waters were also more full of mischief then, with the nightmare of underwater snags adding to the well-founded paranoia of all steamboat captains.

River historians point to well over 400 steamboat calamities on the Missouri River, more than half from downed tree trunk snags piercing the ships' wood hulls. According to the curators of the Arabia Steamboat Museum in Kansas City, it was a fallen walnut tree, with roots embedded in river bottom mud, that led to the demise in 1856 of the steamer *Arabia.*

The *Arabia* hit the snag on the evening of September 5 as porters served a supper. It halted abruptly, lurched upward, then began taking on tons of water. Soon, only upper decks peeked out from the river. A single life boat ferried anxious passengers to a steep embankment on the Missouri shore.

Several hundred tons of cargo, destined for frontier outposts, were lost. The lone fatality was a forgotten mule tied up on a lower deck. Wagons came down from Parkville to take shaken passengers to Mr. Park's hotel for the night. Their rescued valuables were left at river's edge and promptly ransacked and looted over night.

Within a matter of days, the *Arabia* sank into the mire, never to be seen again—until an excavation project began 130 years later. Today, the salvaged contents and remains of the *Arabia* are displayed in a wonderful museum on 400 Grand Avenue in the Kansas City Flea Market area.

A visit to the museum can give you an appreciation for frontier history, ingenuity, tragedy and perseverance. After taking in this tribute to pioneer spirit, consider a trek upriver to the campus of Park University, once the site of the old Park Hotel where the passengers of the ill-fated *Arabia* found comfort.

The university is private, so consult with college officials before entering the grounds. The campus provides excellent views of the river, and if you look south, you may come close to the site of the *Arabia*'s destruction.

There is much to ponder on the hill at Park—our ancestors' hard lives and their resilience. Think of *Arabia*'s passengers with their last belongings looted. This brings to mind an adage of a steamboat captain named Mark Twain: "Each person is born to one possession which outvalues all his others—his last breath."

Pere Marquette State Park

Native Americans saw bald eagles as sacred birds, as protectors of the people. Settlers who established the country of America must have had similar ideas, for in 1782 they made the eagle our national emblem.

Unfortunately, the new Americans did not hold bald eagles in the same reverence as Native Americans. Bald eagles were nearly wiped out in the last century by destruction of their habitat, excessive hunting, and use of harmful chemicals such as DDT.

Major efforts by scientists, wildlife experts and environmentalists have slowly brought eagle populations back from the precipice of extinction. A great place to use as a base to witness the comeback of the American eagle is Pere Marquette State Park, nestled in the bluffs of the Illinois River.

Nothing is quite so magical as a long stay in the lodge or cabins at Pere Marquette State Park in the dead of winter, when crunchy snow covers the ground. Adding to that magic is the presence of almost 2,000 bald eagles that winter up and down the mighty rivers near the park.

Only the Klamath Basin area near the border of Oregon and California can claim more wintering eagles among the lower 48 states. Bluffs and valleys of the Illinois, Mississippi and Missouri rivers adjacent to Pere Marquette make the park a fine roost for humans keen on eagle watching.

From mid-December through late February, Pere Marquette hosts eagle education programs and eagle sightseeing tours. The park education center boasts a kid-friendly, six-foot wide by four-foot deep model eagle's nest, which will put young imaginations in flight.

While the tours can take you to nearby places where eagle sightings are virtually guaranteed, quieter and more solitary quests to see the eagles can take place in the park itself. Walking trails closest to Stump Lake and the Illinois River are the most scenic; are closest to spots where eagles may be seen; and have the added advantage of being among the shortest hikes within the park.

Your best bet for eyeing eagles may be along Goatcliff Trail, which passes a number of fine bluff overlooks before ending at McAdams Peak. At 370 feet above the rivers, McAdams Peak looks west across both the Illinois and Mississippi rivers. In recent years, park rangers have reported eagles' roosts in the trees near McAdams Peak.

If you're a bluff lover, then you have something in common with the eagles. They often make their nests and roost in trees along the bluffs. They use the thermals rising up the bluff sides to soar or to kettle.

Bluffs like those at Pere Marquette are loved by humans for relaxation, reflection and reconnaissance—taking in the view. Imagine what eagles can see from their high bluff perches. Their eyes are eight times stronger than even the best set of the human kind.

PIASA BIRD DELIVERED TERROR

UP FROM ST. LOUIS, JUST NORTH OF THE RIVER CITY OF ALTON, ILL., IS WHERE A BIRD-LIKE MONSTER ONCE TERRORIZED THE MISSISSIPPI RIVER VALLEY. It was called the Piasa (pronounced PIE-a-saw).

European explorers, such as Father Jacques Marquette, first learned of the Piasa legend from a painting of the creature on a bluff wall which they viewed while traveling down the river. Marquette described it as a huge, red-eyed carnivore with sharp talons and long wings mounted on a multi-colored, scaly body.

For the Illini tribes, the Piasa was far more than a cliff-side painting. Its story was a lesson on tribal survival. The tale of the evil Piasa's demise, thanks to the courage of Chief Outaga, has great practical and spiritual value.

Centuries ago, the Piasa wreaked havoc among those living on the bluffs and along the river wetlands. An unwelcome visitor from the south, the reptile-turned-bird would target children and young adults. The creature would swoop down upon them and let off a scream that seemed to paralyze its victims with fear.

The bird was known to carry victims back alive to its lair and to tear them apart, limb by limb, before devouring them. Chief Outaga had enough of the carnage. He hatched a plan in which he would lure the Piasa into a trap using himself as bait.

Outaga assembled his best warriors and asked them to hide in a circle of brush with arrows at the ready. Outaga offered himself up as a sacrifice on a bluff perch within the borders of the brush camouflage.

The chief's warriors urged him to dress in his finest raiment of feathers to confront the monster. Outaga cautioned the warriors that he must be naked and vulnerable. Loud plumage might scare off the Piasa. He also advised that their aim could be lost in a chaos of feathers in a Piasa attack.

Outaga's instincts were correct. The Piasa was attracted to his bare flesh as he crouched in a loin cloth atop the bluff. The Piasa dived for Outaga with talons open, only to be brought down in a hail of arrows. The screeching, mortally wounded Piasa crashed into the Mississippi below.

The legend of the Piasa continues to bring sojourners to the river bluffs between Grafton and Alton, Ill. A visitor who climbs to the top of one of the lofty sandstone spires may find the courage of Outaga. The warmth of his courage is best found in late afternoon on a summer's day. That's when the light is just right.

Close your eyes and feel the sun's warmth on your face. Imagine what thoughts must have passed through the mind of Outaga as he awaited his confrontation with the unknown. He faced death, but a death with meaning.

The lesson of Outaga is one of self-sacrifice for others. Such sacrifice is more likely to be successful when offered in humility—without fanfare, fireworks or feathery plumage.

Pinnacles Offer Lessons for Youth

Like an aging grandmother hidden away somewhere and mostly forgotten, the Pinnacles of central Missouri receive neither the respect nor the recognition they deserve.

The Pinnacles are a precariously thin ridge towering almost 100-feet high and extending more than 1,000 feet along Silver Fork Creek. This formation came into being tens of thousands of years ago when Silver Fork Creek doubled back on itself, crowded nearby Kelly Creek, and squeezed out the precipitous limestone ridge known today as the Pinnacles.

Land north on Highway 63 out of Columbia, Mo., transforms quickly from rolling hills to farmland plain. That's why the Pinnacles are such a geographical delight. They sit in an otherwise flat area about 12 miles north of Columbia, tucked away in dense growth just east of Highway 63.

The isolated grandmother analogy for the Pinnacles is an apt one, for geologists refer to the formation as a "senile ridge" that has only a few thousand years of life remaining. Erosion from top to bottom has taken a toll on the Pinnacles.

The high serrated ridge, which can be covered on foot with a path, narrows to only a few feet wide in several locations. The top ridge has been breached by erosion, and at several points below the ridge there are perforations which have been described as windows or natural arches.

Ironically, the grandmotherly Pinnacles are a magnet for the young. A brochure about the site, produced by Boone County, describes the rocky formation and its trails as forever popular with young romantics.

They have always been a popular destination for college students from Columbia. Indeed, my first encounter on the pathways of the Pinnacles was as a journalism student at the University of Missouri.

Perhaps the great wisdom of the Pinnacles for these young visitors has always been intuitive—lessons that have to do with time and the transitory nature of appearances. The young who climb and carouse and caress on the Pinnacles are fresh, limber and full of life. Their youthful antics are supported by a craggy, weathered grandmother—she tolerates these young as she tolerates junipers and wildflowers growing in her crevices.

A sojourn to the Pinnacles can be a learning experience for any age: learn here that appearances are transitory; learn here that flesh and bone, lichens and limestone, are all destined to fade; learn here that even a rocky ridge can grow old and become senile.

The trick is to wear the wrinkles, age spots, graying hair, the crow's feet as a badge of honor, and to remember that appearances are not everything. There can be a spirit beneath that is more important, that lifts us up and allows us to appreciate all kinds of beauty, even a more sublime beauty transformed by time.

Bluffs of the Warrior Hermann

Missouri land between Defiance on the east and beyond Rhinelander on the west is referred to as the Show Me State's prized wine country.

Vineyards do quite well here, especially on the south faces of the rolling bluffs that together form the northern boundary of this section of Missouri River Valley. Hop-scotching from one welcoming winery to the next on this hilly terrain can make for a very pleasant day, indeed.

This beautiful area is not only wine country, it also is Hermann country. Settlers who came to these hills and valleys in the late 1830s and 1840s were German immigrants intent on preserving their culture and on duplicating their former homeland in Germany's Rhine River Valley.

The settlers, many associated with the German Settlement Society of Philadelphia, bestowed the name of Hermann on their first town in the region. Hermann der Cherusker is one of the legendary heroes of the Germanic tribes of early Europe.

A leader of the Cheruskan tribe, Hermann was raised in Rome about the first century A.D. He turned on his native city as Roman legions under Quinctilius Varus sought to expand Caesar Augustus' empire northward and subdue the Germanic tribes.

In a fierce battle, the outnumbered forces of Hermann destroyed three legions and repulsed the Romans. The victory had great historical significance because it hindered Roman aspirations to rule Germanic regions, and it insured that many Teutonic peoples would be free to govern themselves and to develop independently.

Folks in the Missouri River Valley towns of Dutzow, Augusta, Holstein and Rhinelander may think they live in wine country—and they do—but they also are in the land of Hermann. The ancient warrior was the inspiration for the first settlers who built a new life in a Germanic tradition.

The city of Hermann itself became a prosperous community that today is more Teutonic than many towns in 21st-century Germany. It has one of the largest wineries in the country, many architectural landmarks, and it's the seat for Gasconade County.

When entering wine country from the west on Highway 94, you will know you are also in Hermann country when you see the 400-foot towers of the Rhineland bluffs across the river from Hermann. The bluffs are like the knees of the ancient warrior, Hermann, rising from a bed of verdant bottomland vegetation.

Stop for a while on the bottomland highway to gaze upon the mighty dolomite knees of the warrior, who sprawls above in calm repose, smug in the success of these early settlers who took his name. Then, continue on down the highway to enjoy the fruits of one of the many bluff wineries.

Lift a glass toward the river valley below. Raise a toast to the warrior, Hermann, father of a new land.

BLUFFS AT HISTORIC ROCHEPORT

BLUFFS AT ROCHEPORT ARE IMPRESSIVE IN EVERY SEASON AND FROM ANY NUMBER OF VANTAGE POINTS. The huge rock towers are midway between Columbia and Booneville on a stretch of Missouri River running north to south.

In fall, it's a visual treat to amble with other folks along the Katy Trail, below the bluffs, and to contrast the chalk-white walls of bluff rock with the reds and golds of area foliage.

In the dead of winter, sculptured chunks of river ice and the desolate, frozen shoreline seem to mirror the stark line of bluffs. It's impossible to miss this unique sight if you are traveling east on I-70, perhaps on a trip from Kansas City to St. Louis.

Lewis and Clark came upon the bluffs of Rocheport while paddling up the Missouri River. They found safe harbor just below Moniteau Creek as the heat of summer arrived in June 1804. The explorers noted in their journal that the huge rocks along the river were "very remarkable."

The steep rocks were not the only remarkable thing to be found at what would become Rocheport. Lewis and Clark reported that they were unable to inspect the area closely because of a great number of "ferocious rattlesnakes" crawling among the rocks.

While the rattlers resulted in an abbreviated stay for the explorers, the snakes did not discourage traders, farmers and politicians from settling Rocheport later. Whig Party politicians chose Rocheport for their state convention in 1840, and then nominated the ill-fated William Henry Harrison for U.S. president.

Rocheport thrived as a trade center and steamboat port up until 1861, but the Civil War brought turmoil and devastation to the bluff town. A succession of floods and fires hit the area after the Civil War, and the population declined throughout the 1900s.

Rocheport today is a much quieter place than it was as a bustling river port or as the site of intense political and civil strife. Bikers, hikers and shutterbugs have replaced the fur traders, boatmen, politicians and railroaders of an earlier, rowdier time.

There is something soothing about all this. The political speeches, the war whoops of secessionist raiders, the cries of disaster brought on by fire and flood—they have all dissolved. Left behind is the constant flow of the river. Left behind are these giant rock sentries standing in silence.

Think Ozymandias. These ancient bluffs, these solidly stacked shelves of rock are nature's Ozymandias. In the poem "Ozymandias," the Romantic writer Percy Bysshe Shelley relates how a monstrous stone statue, weathered and beaten by wind and storm, is all that's left of the empire of the great Egyptian king of kings.

Of course, not all is abandoned at Rocheport. A delightful little village remains. And at night, the moon and stars come out, to reflect light upon the bluffs and to twinkle in the river.

Unique Bluffs & Overlooks 51

CCC Legacy Left on Mudlick Bluffs

A hike to the scenic overlooks in Sam A. Baker Park affords more than the usual reward of beautiful Ozark vistas. Three rustic shelters of stone and timber can be found high on the park's Mudlick Mountain Wild Area.

The first shelter I discovered on a Sam A. Baker hike had an open face that looked out on the verdant valley of Big Creek and its gravel bars below. A sturdy structure, it had fireplaces at each end for winter comfort. What a perfect find, and escape, this could be from the cold of a January hike.

Shelters on the Mudlick Mountain bluffs inspire admiration for all the young fellows who toiled on them in the 1930s as building projects for the Civilian Conservation Corps (CCC).

Many of our most shrill propagandists and ideologues have convinced us that nothing worthy or lasting can be wrought by any government work program. These blowhards need to take a hike—literally—to see the work of the CCC men at Sam A. Baker and other parks in the region.

The CCC program began in 1933 with the Emergency Conservation Act. Its purpose was two-fold: to ease the unemployment crisis facing young men in the Great Depression; to restore and conserve national forests and soil resources. The development of protected state and national parks became part of the mission.

CCC camps usually consisted of a 200-man crew. Camp periods lasted about six months. Sam A. Baker benefitted greatly from five camp periods.

The CCC camps of Sam A. Baker were responsible for putting up phone lines and installing water. They built bridges, cabins, latrines, stables and more. They started a dining hall that was finished later by the Works Progress Administration (WPA).

Sam A. Baker is just one example of the enriching and enduring CCC handiwork. In 1985, a half century after the program, almost 250 buildings and 95 structures in the Missouri state park system were included in a unique nomination to the National Register of Historic Places.

Check out the lodge, stone hiking shelters, picnic pavilion and the 1,000 Steps Trail at Washington State Park. All were built by African American CCC stonemasons in rugged terrain.

Check out the rustic architecture built by CCC craftsmen at Meramec State Park. Comfortable shelters and outdoor facilities melt into a rugged, natural landscape.

Across the Mississippi River north of St. Louis, check out the retreats, lookouts and trails built by CCC men at Pere Marquette State Park with its massive, beautiful stone lodge.

Call them the "welfare kings" of President Franklin Roosevelt's New Deal, if you wish. But I appreciate the cabins, hideaways and climbs these CCC men have built. They have left behind a wonderful wilderness refuge—a refuge, in part, from the ideologues and blowhards of civilization.

Magical Bluffs Made for Sunsets

Many tall bluffs along Missouri's Meramec River are worth a climb for the vistas they provide beyond the river valley below. Bluffs located just a few miles southwest of the city of St. Louis—part of the Sunset Hills chain along the lower Meramec—are of historical note and natural import.

The line of bluffs on the east side of the Meramec, north of the I-44 river bridge, were once the land of Edwin Lemp, son of the St. Louis Brewery family. Not long out of college in 1909, Lemp found this area a picturesque spot for pitching a tent and camping.

Lemp was fascinated by the animal and insect life on the bluffs, including the migrating Monarch butterflies, which would cover the bluffs in early October and again in May on their round-trips to and from Mexico. Lemp's favorite camping spot became the site of his estate, which he built for himself and named "Cragwold" for the rocky cliffs in the area.

An outdoorsman who disassociated himself from the family beer business, Lemp brought new animals to the long stretch of river bluffs and the 12,500-square-foot home that he constructed on the edge of the bluffs. Some of those animals, such as fallow deer, still roam the area.

The heavily wooded acreage and Lemp Estate were bought in 1975 by noted real estate developer Russell Emmenegger. Nearby residents were fearful the Meramec hills and bluffs would succumb to a suburban home development. But Emmenegger gave almost 95 acres of the tract to the city of Kirkwood for his namesake park.

Hikers can view the rolling Ozark foothills for more than 30 miles from the Meramec Bluffs of the park. It is not the same view, however, as was afforded Native Americans who came to the hills after visiting the salt licks along the Meramec centuries ago.

The expansive views are marred today by warehouses, an industrial park, a sprawling Chrysler auto plant and a roaring Interstate 44 that often clogs at rush hour. Sometimes a long plume of coal smoke from the power plant in Labadie is clearly visible.

Still, the overlooks of what is now Emmenegger Park are worth a hike. They are worth it, if only to imagine what once was, and to see what now remains. And there is still the magic of those migratory Monarch butterflies, which alight on the Meramec Bluffs in late spring and early fall on their 2,000-mile journeys.

A trek to Emmenegger on the right day may bring a fluttering orange-winged Monarch your way. If one lands on your hand, know well that you are witness to a miracle of nature.

The Aztecs once believed Monarchs were infused with wandering souls of fallen warriors. Monarchs, however, do not wander. Their homing system is infallible—and no one knows how it works. Monarchs at Emmenegger tell us that life need not be wholly understood to be fully appreciated.

Overlooking a Trail of Tears

The forced removal of Cherokees from their ancestral lands consti-
tutes one of the saddest and darkest chapters in American history.
You may encounter a portion of this painful history at the Trail of Tears State
Park north of Cape Girardeau.

Cherokee families were driven out of their homelands of Tennessee and
Georgia to less verdant territory in Oklahoma. The lengthy route of their forced
migration took them through Illinois and Missouri.

American patriot Davy Crockett denounced the Indian Removal Act in
Congress. Daniel Webster advised the Cherokees to appeal their removal to the
U.S. Supreme Court, where they received a favorable hearing.

President Andrew Jackson dissed the judiciary and challenged courts to try
to enforce any rulings for Native Americans. He advised the whites to "build a
fire under them. When it gets hot enough, they'll go!"

The bluffs at Trail of Tears State Park stand sentry over the site of the
Cherokee crossing at the Mississippi River. By the time the Cherokees reached
the river banks in December 1838, the ragged exiles had buried many women,
children and elderly.

Their route through Kentucky and Illinois was especially difficult. An early
blizzard of frozen rain, sleet and snow spawned pneumonia. Local whites
refused to allow their encampments, while others took their horses and live-
stock as forced payment for "damage" done along the travel route.

Cherokee detachments endured brutal conditions while marooned on the
river banks across from Cape Girardeau County. The Mississippi was packed
with grotesque chunks of ice crashing, then groaning, in a slush flow south. The
emaciated Cherokees, numbed with cold, had to somehow make it west,
beyond the river peril.

Go to the Trail of Tears Bluffs and look across to the banks on the east side of
the river. Imagine the sight of thousands of stranded Cherokees. Imagine the sound
of low wails, plaintive cries, a biblical gnashing of teeth. Imagine the bluffs on which
you stand as the last vision to be seen by a Cherokee before eyes closed forever.

It took most of January 1839 to get the Cherokee across the river in two sets
of boats. The river toll was heavy. More than 4,000 Cherokees lost their lives—
one-fifth of their population—before they reached the final destination set for
them near Fort Gibson, Okla.

Go to the Trail of Tears Bluffs and look down upon the ghosts of those
Cherokee. It is said that no people had better use of their five senses than these
children of the wilderness.

Imagine the pain endured with their heightened senses. Look to the heavens
and ask to experience the senses of these same children of the wilderness.
Perhaps the blessing of a new moral sensitivity could end such outrages as were
committed on a trail of tears.

Truman Lake's Sun-Kissed Bluffs

To write about Missouri bluffs with no mention of Midwest rock climbers would constitute the commission of a great omission. Limestone, sandstone, rhyolite or granite, if it comes stacked in a heap, they'll scale it.

Scribes and poets aside, no one ever becomes more intimate with the crags and crannies of bluffs than rock climbers. Within climbing clubs, you'll find rock huggers who are every bit as committed to the welfare of Mother Nature as any wild-eyed tree hugger.

Even so, rock climbers often get a bad rap. They're branded as careless daredevils; scorned as irresponsible trespassers; dissmissed as outdoor pests, who are likely to deface cliff, cave and boulder as part of their sport.

My experience with rock climbers has been quite the contrary. As a feature writer accompanying these bluff dwellers, my impression is that truly dedicated ropers and rappellers exhibit an excess of awareness, environmental concern, energy, courtesy and trustworthiness.

Of course, rock climbers also are a font of knowledge about bluffs in the state. A popular guide for those who like to edge upon a ledge is *Climber's Guide to the Midwest's Metamorphic Forms,* by Marcus Floyd.

Floyd's fine guide to the top spots, which is richly illustrated and finely detailed, is fun to look at even if you have no intention of doing any face climbing yourself. And it's a sure bet you'll catch his enthusiasm for high places, even if you have little desire to get to the summits the hard way.

Truman Lake Bluffs are among the rock towers of Missouri that Floyd singles out as worthy of a climber's interest. Many of the bluffs seem to sprout out from the lake itself—a unique delight for a climber's belay man or a sight-seeing layman.

Bullfrogs, jumping fish and floundering turtles will be among your aquatic companions, should you venture out on the lower ledges of the bluffs. These nearby critters are part of what makes the bluff area unique.

Dead, dormant, sun-bleached trees occasionally poke out from Truman Lake near the shoreline of the bluffs. The stark branches provide a resting spot for water fowl that cruise the waters for an easy bite to eat.

You don't have to be a climber to get a thrill from a trip to Truman. A number of trails provide access to the bluffs, as well as to caves, woods, savannahs and wetlands in the area. If you are a confirmed hiker, don't let that keep you from commingling with any climbers who might be close.

Climbers have their own special wisdom to impart. They'll tell you it's the challenge, not the risk, that's behind a bluff climb. Risk-takers need not apply. They're not welcome.

Especially admirable for all who enjoy nature's bounty is the climbers' leave-no-trace-behind ethic. This may just seem like common sense, but sadly it's not always common practice.

CANOEISTS' FAVORITE: VILANDER BLUFF

YOU CAN GET A CONVINCING ARGUMENT FROM THE MERAMEC CANOE CROWD THAT VILANDER BLUFF IS THE MOST SPECTACULAR SIGHT IN MISSOURI. Vilander's towering rock fortress is 10 miles down the river from the magnificent Onondaga Cave.

Landlubbers will be hard put to argue with the paddlers, because the Vilander area is not easily accessible for hikers. At some point, a trail may be established by the state to the site. For now, Vilander is best reached—and appreciated—by canoe.

The 200-foot cliff is a visual reward and natural landmark for those who love to float between Onondaga Cave and Meramec State Park. Among such veteran paddlers is Roger Taylor, who often puts his canoe in Meramec waters at Castlewood, which he calls home.

Vilander is a favorite of Taylor's. He talks about it with reverence. It's a wilderness vision that helped inspire his battle for a Missouri Scenic Rivers Act in 1970. Taylor's idea was to get state protection for the picturesque, spring-fed, free-flowing rivers and their banks in the Missouri Ozarks.

Taylor headed a petition drive to get the measure on the ballot. Under his plan, state zoning would protect land for 300 feet from either side of the stream shore. It would be protected from commercial development, littering, pollution and erosion due to bad forestry and land practices.

All of this seems pretty reasonable, but some rural landowners had their own ideas about the initiative. They called it communism. They didn't like canoeists. They didn't like the notion of the state limiting use of their land for aesthetic and recreation purposes.

Not only did Taylor lose the scenic initiative battle, but late one night during the campaign his car exploded as it sat in his driveway. Who would have thought that reverence for natural places could get you dynamited?

Taylor was unpleasantly surprised, but undaunted. While he and his environmental allies lost the scenic rivers battle, they were organized to fight another day. They succeeded a decade later in stopping the Meramec Dam project, which would have put many natural wonders under water.

Taylor—and his favorite scenery of the Vilander Bluff area—can be an inspiration for future fighters for our natural heritage. There can never be enough inspiration for those fighting for open space, for wildlife protection, for erosion control, for ecological and environmental integrity.

There is much to ponder on a visit to Vilander. It's especially hard not to be inspired by the gnarly 500-year-old cedars that cling to its sheer ledges. How have they survived so many years in wind and storm, ice and snow, drought as well as deluge?

If those cedars can take root in the scant soil of Vilander's rocky crevices, surely we can take our own stand for nature. Like these trees of Vilander, let us hold onto what the earth has given us with unflinching tenacity.

WASHINGTON STATE PARK

THUNDERBIRDS WERE ONCE IN GREAT QUANTITY ALONG THE DOLOMITE BLUFFS TOWERING OVER THE BIG RIVER IN WASHINGTON STATE PARK. In fact, a few of the birds can still be found in the park's petroglyph preservation area.

Thunderbirds are mythical bird-like creatures with squared shoulders and triangular bodies. The head faces sideways while the bottom feathers, or tail, fan outward. Archeologists believe these birds were symbols of rain and fertility for Mississippians, a Native American culture that once thrived in the Midwest river valleys.

There is a mystical quality to the thunderbirds and other petroglyph art at Washington State Park. The word "petroglyph" derives from the Greek words *paetros*, meaning stone, and *glyphe*, for carving or sculpted image. The park site may have the largest set of petroglyphs in the state.

A brochure at the state park office titled, "Talking Thunderbirds," provides artist recreations of what the 1,000-year-old petroglyphs may have looked like before erosion took its toll. In addition to the magical birds, there are fertility ovals or eggs, arrows, tribesmen, coiled snakes, lightning bolts, shamanic maces and more.

Archeologists can only theorize as to what the original Mississippian artists were trying to say with their symbols. Were they chronicles of specific events from eons ago? Were they recordings of shamanic rituals to be followed? Were they warnings to some future civilization about life or death?

One way to enhance the experience of a sitting on the Big River Bluffs is to first check out the petroglyphs left by the artisans who once lived in this wilderness area. Then, hike to the solid and solitary gazebo anchored on the overlook above the valley of the Big River.

Near the gazebo, a wide array of outcroppings are available to choose from as you consider where to take a rest. Be careful. Be wise. Select a site where you can zone out comfortably—without the worry of being too close to disaster's edge.

Imagine the comfortable lifestyle of the Mississippians below you. They are sunning and swimming on the gravel bars of the Big River. They are catching catfish, bluegill and bass, as anglers still do today from the river below. Mississippians were blessed with an ideal life, but anthropologists say they suddenly disappeared from the region. No one seems to know why they left or where they went.

Imagine what those petroglyphs were supposed to say, as you also contemplate the fate of the first residents of this fertile land of milk and honey.

I have sat on Big River's bluffs and contemplated the work of our own civilization's petroglyph makers. At Yucca Mountain, Nev., they must design symbolic warnings for future civilizations. The symbols must warn about our radioactive waste—deadly for centuries—buried at Yucca.

Who will read these modern petroglyphs? Will they be understood?

SAD HISTORY BELOW WESTON BLUFFS

ON THE NORTHWEST MISSOURI BORDER, OVERLOOKING RICH BOTTOMLAND FOR-
EST AND HISTORIC LEAVENWORTH, KAN., ARE THE MAGNIFICENT, TREE-LINED
RIVER BLUFFS OF WESTON.

Meriwether Lewis and William Clark reached Weston on their way up the
Missouri River in July 1804. They recorded evidence of an abandoned Kansa
tribe village in their journals.

The land on the west side of the river became known to Americans as the
frontier territory of Kansas. In 1827, Fort Leavenworth was founded in the
Kansas Territory. On the Missouri side, the town of Weston began to grow with
an economy based on tobacco, hemp and western trade.

The Missouri River double-crossed Weston in 1858 with a major channel
shift that destroyed its port. The town saw further calamity after the Civil War,
but it has undergone a revival in recent times thanks to Kansas City folks looking for a day-trip getaway.

The bluffs overlooking Kansas and the wily Missouri River are found in
Weston Bend State Park, just south of the town. Much has happened on the
Kansas land below the bluffs—which remains home to Fort Leavenworth.

This land was home to troops who periodically escorted traders along the Santa
Fe Trail. This land saw exercises by Buffalo Soldiers, the famed all-black 10th
Cavalry Unit. This land was the site of exile for Chief Joseph and 700 of his Nez
Perce tribe members after their humiliating surrender to the U.S. Cavalry.

The Nez Perce were not double-crossed by a river, but they certainly were
cheated out of their ancestral lands by a succession of U.S. treaties forced upon
them. After a series of skirmishes, Chief Joseph tried to flee with his people to a
sanctuary in Canada, but was stopped by cavalry.

In 1877, Chief Joseph and several hundred surviving Nez Perce were held
captive at Leavenworth, before being sent to an Oklahoma reservation that was
far from their original native lands in the U.S. Northwest.

If you take an interest in the fate of our great land's first inhabitants, take a
trip to Weston Bend Bluffs for some reflection. You might consider taking *The
Wisdom of Native Americans,* edited by Kent Nerburn, on your trip.

Chief Joseph's account of his people's suffering at Leavenworth is included in
Nerburn's book. He notes the many forked tongues of the white "law chiefs"
who decided their future.

Today, Chief Joseph is hailed as one of the wisest Native Americans ever. In
the chief's own time, Buffalo Bill Cody called him "the greatest American Indian
ever produced."

Among Chief Joseph's observations on the white man: "We were like deer.
They were like grizzly bears. . . . We were contented to let things remain as the
Great Spirit made them. They were not, and would change the rivers and the
mountains if they did not suit them."

STREAMS AND SPRINGS

GREAT RIVERS OF NORTH AMERICA—THE ILLINOIS, THE MISSOURI, THE OHIO, THE MISSISSIPPI—MEET, MIX, ROLL AND ROIL WITH EACH OTHER IN THE UNDULATING VALLEYS OF THE MISSOURI REGION.

Along these primal waterways, hills and bluffs offer panoramic views of the river giants as they move onward and swell with their many tributaries. Additional vantage points to gaze upon the powerful rivers have been made available through the hand of man.

For example, a bike route on the new Page Avenue Bridge, which links St. Louis and St. Charles counties, offers a commanding view of the Missouri River as it heads northeast to meet up with the Mississippi.

A viewing deck on public land at Confluence Point, several miles north of downtown St. Louis, allows visitors to see where the Missouri empties into the Mississippi. This also is the site where Lewis and Clark began their epic adventure up the Big Muddy to the lands of the Sioux, Blackfeet, Shoshone and Nez Perce.

By far, this writer's most favored man-made observation point is on the old Chain of Rocks Bridge. The worn Highway 66 bridge, now dedicated to pedestrian traffic, spans the wide Mississippi just a few miles south of its intersection with the Missouri River in the Columbia Bottoms area.

Water coming under the old bridge from the north runs smooth and full of force. On the south side of the bridge, the water suddenly turns turbulent, smashing into a chain of rocks where it bubbles and boils, froths and foams. The sight of the water's churning metamorphosis is both memorable and transforming.

Great rivers are natural forces to enjoy and to contemplate from high perches. At some point, however, it is essential to climb down from hill, bluff and bridge for a river encounter that is more up close and personal.

Soft sandy shorelines and jagged rock peninsulas allow pathfinders to view the region's great rivers from every perspective. If a river can actually be a "Great Brown God," as Missouri's prodigal poet, Thomas Eliot, once declared, then a river should be contemplated from every perspective available.

Of course, Missouri nature lovers have always known that glimpses of the Infinite can be found not just in a continent's big brown rivers but also in the region's more modest streams, springs and falls; its wetlands and its shut-ins; its abundant water features.

Water sites are places for solitary reflection and communal celebration. Water flows to shape lands, to smooth boulders, to cool the body, and to calm the mind. With time, humankind has observed water's ability to wear away hard rock and mineral. So, it should come as no surprise that man calls upon the water to wash away his worst fears as well as the worst of his transgressions.

Water is the unquestioned creator and ultimate destroyer; it is the yin and the yang; it gives life and it takes life away. Water can be loved almost amorously for its pure and simple physicality, and it can be worshiped at the same time for its transcendent spirituality.

All those who comprehend the varied characteristics of water should be pleased with the small but sensational sample of water sites selected for inclusion in this volume. Several of these prime selections are, naturally, from the area of the Ozark National Scenic Riverways.

Thousands of canoeists, who have floated the clear waters of the Current and Jacks Fork, will easily understand why certain nooks along these Ozark rivers count as natural wonders. Missouri's best artists have certainly understood the great magic of Ozark waters. Thomas Hart Benton's rich and colorful inland riverscapes reveal his intimacy with the enchanting haunts of southern Missouri's Ozark frontier.

Among these haunts are the many springs that service the Current and Jacks Fork. Springs provide a hint of the invisible waterworld beneath the ground. Nothing inspires natural wonder like the constant flow from gushing earth cavities. In winter, these sites steam like some strange and wonderful outdoor sauna. In summer, their chilly waters can give a refreshing jolt to body and soul.

The largest spring on the Jacks Fork flows some 14 miles upstream from the river's juncture with the Current. Known as Alley Spring, its waters support islands of bright green watercress—emerald eye candy that shows what it really means on this earth to be green.

Springs on the Current River are many and varied. There's Welch Spring and Cave Spring and Pulltite Spring and Round Spring and Blue Spring. All the springs are unique energy sites guaranteed to create lifelong memories when properly appreciated. Take time to ponder the copper blue pond at Blue Spring and you'll never wonder again about what it really means to be true blue.

If springs evoke the mysteries of what lies below, the small canyons and shut-ins of Missouri at dusk surely prompt wonder at the canopy of constellations that twirl above. Rocky shut-ins provide phenomenal observatory posts and will serve to convert many visitors into amateur astronomers.

This writer will never forget an all-night experience at the Castor River Shut-ins—a gorgeous, gleaming moon reflected on the rocks, the river and its hopscotch series of pools. Then, without warning, the moon was swallowed in a lunar eclipse. Artist Ed Thias captures perfectly the cosmic scene produced by that eclipse.

Shut-ins along rivers and streams are tailor-made to accommodate gatherings of earthlings who love the moon and stars. There's something special about a literal circle of friends joined together in awe of the night sky while seated around a blazing fire. There's nothing impertinent or sacrilegious, however, with breaking the friendly circle to find a private spot beneath the stars for solitary contemplation.

Of course, shut-ins take on a different character in the light of day. They become nature's water parks. They become filled with the chatter and laughter of youngsters who have arrived to enjoy the slippery chutes, slides and cascades of natural shut-ins. Their parents sometimes cannot resist becoming part of the watery horseplay.

The blue-gray canyons and gorges of Johnson's Shut-ins are formed by some of the oldest exposed rock on the planet. Even a cursory understanding of the geology of these shut-ins provides so very much to think about. It's simply awesome to climb into the steep wilderness above the shut-ins to gaze down upon children at play. Their play is among boulders traced to rock and lava from volcanoes erupting more than a billion years ago.

Despite encroaching civilization, there are still so many special places, sacred sites, and natural wonders to find and enjoy. Because of civilization and its many discontents, there has never been a greater need to "get away from it all" and to reconnect with nature, with "Gaia," with the Earth Goddess—whatever you choose to call it.

A need to head to woods, spring and stream is especially felt by conservationists, ecologists and environmentalists. This author's modest environmental activism finds expression in signing petitions, sending out checks to advocacy groups, sending letters to politicians, as well as teaching and writing about environmental protection issues.

Retreats to natural settings are essential respites from these activities. However, the journeys always come full circle. It becomes necessary to return to signing petitions, sending out checks to environmental groups, sending letters to politicians, as well as teaching and writing about the defense of nature. The environment needs defending.

Just a few months after the profile on Johnson's Shut-ins was written, that beautiful spot was devastated by unprecedented calamity. On the morning of Dec. 14, 2005, the wall of an electric utility reservoir atop nearby Proffit Mountain collapsed. The AmerenUE reservoir for Taum Sauk hydroelectric station released more than 1 billion gallons of water.

The deluge uprooted trees, washed out giant rocks, denuded riverbanks and covered much of the area of Johnson Shut-ins with sand and sediment. The disaster would have likely resulted in many deaths and serious injuries had it occurred during the summer recreation season.

Assessments of the environmental damage, investigations into possible negligence by the utility, and the outcome of related lawsuits remained uncertain at the time this book went to press. What is certain is that if we are to preserve our natural wonders, we must all demand better stewardship and more accountability for the protection of the environment.

Still another disturbing story broke just as this book was going to press. A study by the U.S. Geological Service found that the spring-fed Jacks Fork River was contaminated with worsening levels of E coli and fecal coliform. The study pointed to commercial trail ride and horse-riding groups as the culprit.

The Missouri Coalition for the Environment immediately argued that any further degradation of the Jacks Fork's waters through overuse and lax management should not be tolerated. Again, it's clear the natural environment needs defending.

This book's primary mission is to inspire and instruct on how to enjoy the natural environment rather than to act as an inducement to fret about all the things that threaten nature. Even so, it may simply be impossible to avoid the conversion to an advocate or caretaker for the outdoor environment after encountering its many natural wonders.

Alley Spring: Jack Fork's Jewel

Alley Spring campground is the point of origin for literally thousands of canoe trips annually on the Ozark National Scenic Riverways. It's a pity, but many of the eager floaters never actually visit the spring for which this embarcation point is named.

I know this is true, because I used to be one of those canoeists who failed to value the importance or the beauty of this magnificent spring. It's the largest on a beautiful coil of winding river known as the Jacks Fork.

In my impatience to get the fun of a canoe trip started, I never took time to visit the spring, or the bright red Alley Spring Roller Mill, or the hiking trail along some of the best natural scenery in river country.

Only in my later years of floating did I cross over the Hwy. 106 bridge from the gravel bar and camping area to see the spring. There are plenty of reasons to make the hike to visit what was once "The Alley Community."

First of all, the surging water flow—more than 80 million gallons daily—helps a canoeist understand why the lower Jacks Fork is floatable all year-round. It keeps the water up. By contrast, upper Jacks Fork can become entirely too shallow in dry stretches of summer and fall.

You don't, however, have to be a canoeist to appreciate the flow of H_2O at Alley Spring. You don't need to be an engineer to marvel at the mill with its water-powered turbine. Belts and driveshafts once took power from the spinning turbine to the milling and sifting machines.

From the 1860s to the 1920s, the mill machinery ground many barrels of flour. The mill became a gathering place. A small school was founded and a community thrived. It was named for John Alley, an earlier settler.

Frequent flooding and, finally, the new technology of industrialization took a toll on Alley Spring. The mill operation became obsolete as Ozark farmers gave up the grain mill for the convenience of the country store.

Fortunately, nature never grows obsolete—and it's still in abundance along a hiking trail circling the mill area. Ferns and flowery columbine cling to clammy rock walls above the spring. Beyond the spring, islands of bright green watercress somehow find anchor on the surface of the rush of water. Below the surface, shiny silver minnows dart this way and that.

Float trippers, amateur engineers, rural historians and naturalists can all find reasons to enjoy time at Alley Spring. However, the nostalgia buff, with a mind for imagining the past, may enjoy Alley Spring the most.

Imagine a bustling mill scene on a fall afternoon in the late 1800s. As dusk arrives, final rays of sun dance off leaves of red and gold. Farmers sit and whittle, but their conversation is muffled by the sound of water and the groan of the mill works. Oh, if only it were possible to trade the sprawl of the mall for the spill of the mill.

BAKER/OZARK DIVE ROCKS

YOU KNOW IT'S SUMMER IN THE OZARKS WHEN THE TRILL OF TINY TOADS AND THE CHUG OF BLIMPY BULLFROGS COMBINE IN A NOISY EVENING CACOPHONY.

You know it's summer in the Ozarks when the repetitive night call of whip-poor-will fills the river valleys and echoes across the forest floor.

You know it's summer in the Ozarks when ankles itch with chiggers, and loathsome ticks must be uprooted from private real estate.

You know it's summer in the Ozarks when heavy river valley fogs are burned off by morning sun well before the first campfire coffee brews.

You know it's summer in the Ozarks when you hear youthful dares over steep dives—dives from river boulders and cliffs that loom high above swiftly flowing currents.

Across the Ozarks, summer finds youthful stuntmen daring and diving into the cold waters of such rivers as St. Francois, Current, Black, Jacks Fork, Eleven Point, Osage, Gasconade and Big Piney and Little Piney.

Nothing compares to the youthful chatter of "dare ya" and "double dare ya," as the pint-sized Super Men and Wonder Women work up the courage for suspended swan dives and ignominious belly flops into Ozark waters.

How do they work up this courage? How do they get to the point where they're ready to soar like hawks or to smash into the water like some bloated amphibian? How do they reach that hair-trigger point when the feet leave muddy rock platforms and meet a rush of liberating air?

An Ozark stream-diving pro turned champion yarn-spinner, aptly named Grady Jim Robinson, once provided me with some insight into how these dives evolve. A country writer of some renown, Grady Jim tells the tale of a great diving contest in which he beat the bully of his county.

According to Grady Jim, diving contests took place every summer on cliffs overlooking the Ozark "crick" in the rural area where he grew up. Trouble was, the county bully always took honors with his double-backflip dive that no one could match.

Grady Jim took up the challenge to best the bully of the county, but he knew it would not be enough just to emulate the blowhard's double backflip. When the contest day arrived, the boys and girls along the river banks once again gasped at the aeronautics of the bully boy. How could he be beat?

Grady Jim dived high into the air, while a friend threw him a candy bar in mid-air. It was all part of the now legendary Ozark double-backflip-eat-a-Snickers-before-you-hit-the-water dive. Grady Jim's slick trick at the "crick" won over the hearts of the girls and the adulation of his buddies.

Nothing is as natural as the whoops and hollers of kids in a diving competition on an Ozark stream. Except, maybe, for the rising chorus of toads and bullfrogs when a noisy diving day must give way to nightfall.

A Natural Gift: Bennett Spring

Missouri is a kinder, gentler state—for the most part. Its hills are soft and rolling; its forests offer inviting refuge; its streams usually flow lazily; its weather is most often moderate, if at times fickle and changeable.

This is not to say that folks, who like "to take it to extremes," are out of luck for finding open-air challenges in the state. Missouri actually has its share of horror stories about knave adventurers—fools who have taken needless gambles in the outdoors and lost with an unfortunate finality.

Nature activities don't have to be matters of life and death. Long hikes in the wilderness should not begin at dusk as thunderstorms build. Cave explorations should not commence without proper equipment, including backup flashlights. Safety is just a matter of common sense.

Even so, all outdoor enthusiasts like to push the envelope. Testing the limits; seeking out the psychological brink; finding the pain threshold—all can be part of the fun of being outward bound. It's fun manifested in a myriad of ways—and you find it:

• In a kayaker who enters frothy whitewater after spring storms.
• In an angler who leaves a warm bed at 3 a.m. for a fishing expedition.
• In a backpacker who disappears into the backwoods for three days.
• In a rock climber whose reach always exceeds his grasp.

There does come a point when the daredevil should pull back; when the temptation to take risks should be quelled. That point can come naturally when it's time to introduce a new generation to outdoor magic.

Turning young people on to nature is tricky, at best, in this time when their attention is drawn to computer screens, video games and iPod tunes. A sure way to turn them off to nature is to make an outdoor experience into a test, a hurdle, a gauntlet. Instead, make the outdoors a gift for them.

Bennett Spring near Lebanon can be that gift. It's a kinder, gentler, kid-friendly park—and a great place to get the young fry hooked on fishing. Youngsters will enjoy dallying along the spring pool, only to discover the park hatchery teeming with trout.

Let that discovery be theirs. Praise them for finding those fish first. Grab fishing licenses at the park store, if the nature neophytes are eager to join the other anglers wading into the water to cast for rainbow trout.

If the kids aren't biting on the idea of fishing, don't force them. A secret to outdoors' success with kids is to be prepared for alternative activities. A net and screw-top jar are handy for bug hunting. A visual scavenger hunt for flora and fauna can be aided with magnifying glasses and binoculars.

The 3,100 acres at Bennett Spring State Park offer bluffs, glades, forests and caves for that first youthful outdoor encounter. Make the visit a present to the young, and you'll find it's a gift that can't be broken or lost.

Big Explanations for Big Spring

ONE OF THE BEST WAYS TO SEE NATURE IS THROUGH THE EYES OF A CHILD. Part of the joy of children is to watch their eyes grow wide as they encounter some new marvel in the outdoors.

That new marvel could be a fluttering butterfly, a walking stick or a bouncy spider spinning its web. Or, it could be an inanimate object that switches on a youngster's sense of wonder. The new marvel could be an opaque quartz crystal or a contorted husk of wood resembling a troll.

In Missouri, that new marvel could be one of more than a thousand springs that bubble, gurgle or roar to the surface. Each and every natural spring has its own identity, character and history. Some exit caves; some flow over slick, moss-covered boulders; some create lush gardens of green that float in their shallows.

The mother of all springs in the great state of Missouri will always be the Big Spring. It is ranked as the biggest such water feature in the United States, and among the largest in the world. Its daily flow averages 280 million gallons, but several histories of the spring claim its hard water flow has at times reached 750 million gallons of gushing crystal water.

Native Americans reportedly called it "a spring that roars." Naturally, this description sparked the interest of American settlers. They clawed their way through rugged terrain to record its existence in about 1803.

Two centuries later, Big Spring is now a protected park and a portion of the federal Ozark National Scenic Riverways. It has a lodge, rustic cabins, and several trails that pass where Native Americans camped, fished and hunted more than 10,000 years ago.

Big Spring is likely to inspire the same questions among young visitors as were posed by settlers discovering the area almost 200 years ago: Where does all this water come from? How come it never runs out? Why does it stay so cold in the midst of summer's heat?

Some frontiersmen hypothesized that Big Spring water came from the Great Lakes or from great unknown bodies of water even farther north. Imagine Lake Michigan draining out of this Missouri hole, hundreds of miles to the Great Lake's south. This would certainly explain the endless supply of water and its cold temperature.

Should you be in the company of inquisitive youngsters when visiting Big Spring, ask them what they think of the frontier explanation for its cold and infinite flow. If that explanation doesn't wash for them, ask them for their own formulations for the origins of this eternally flowing fount.

Curiosity may kill cats, but it needn't silence kids. Keep them guessing as to where these millions of gallons come from. Does it all come from a giant bathtub yet to be discovered?

In fact, Big Spring is thought to drain the rain from much of the area within 50 radial miles. Come to think of it, that's a mighty big bathtub!

Brilliant Ozark Blue Spring

The Missouri Ozarks has literally hundreds of springs, mammoth and miniscule, but none so remarkable as Blue Spring near the Current River. No running water anywhere can match the intensity and depth of blue emanating from this spring.

The Osage Tribe dubbed this special earth fountain as the "Spring of the Summer Sky." Native Americans counseled that it is best to capture the spring's singular spectrum of color on a brilliant and hot summer day.

There is much speculation as to why Blue Spring sets the standard for inland blue water sources of North America. Some say it's because the spring is bottomless—with an explored depth of 250 feet. Others say it's because of the light refraction on tiny mineral and organic particles suspended in its watery depths.

Blue Spring was once a site where Native Americans set up camp thousands of years B.C. The encampments gave way to a trading post of white settlers in the 1800s. More than a few legends have sprung from this spring among folks in Ozark hill country, beyond the intersection of the Jacks Fork and Current rivers.

One such tall tale from the late 1800s involves a timberman whose blind mule stumbled and fell from a steep wooded cliff above the spring. The woodsman, fearing he had lost the transportation half of his turn-of-the-century work force, ran to the edge of Blue Spring Bluff to find his mule enjoying the icy cold water.

The story goes that the woodsman joined his mule for relief from the tropical heat that afflicts the area in August. This writer first enjoyed the waters of Blue Spring on a canoe trip with college buddies. A swimming companion was found in an angry mink, rather than a grateful mule.

My brief encounter in Blue Spring waters was inspired by a bet that I could not stay in the spring and count to 20. The wager was won, but at a sobering price—the winner emerged almost as blue as the spring itself.

You can find Blue Spring by heading east from the town of Eminence on Highway 106. After crossing the Current River, look for a gravel road on the right, which leads to a walking trail to Blue Spring. The preferred route to the spring is by canoe on the Current past Twin Rivers.

Blue Spring itself is less accessible today than when this writer was in college. To preserve the deep spring's integrity, state conservationists have built walkways and an observation platforms to view the blue.

Blue Spring is another special site that counsels contemplation rather than calculation. What makes the water so blue? A better on-site question: Why are such issues important?

Blue Spring's waters are for dreaming. Drink in these lapis lazuli colors of Blue Spring for a rescue and a respite from your life's work—be it physical or mental.

Castor River Shut-Ins

For sunning, dipping, wading and swimming in a scenic environment, you'll be hard-pressed to find a better place than the Castor River Shut-ins—known to locals as "Pink Rocks."

Situated like a pink diamond in the rough, somewhere between the village of Fredericktown and the tiny town of Yount, Castor River Shut-ins is a short trail hike from a parking area marked as the Amidon Memorial Conservation Area. Long before you near the end of the trail, you'll be amazed to hear the roar of the river over the rocks.

Castor currents ebb and flow, bubble and blow, through a virtual rock garden. Nature's whirling waters have carved out and smoothed out some rock-solid foot rests, easy chairs, couches and king-size beds. This waterproof furniture can be used for dangling feet, lounging half-submerged in cool bubbly or for sunning like a turtle.

It's tempting to close your eyes and just listen to the audio performance echoing within the pink rock canyons of the Castor. Open your eyes, and you'll drink in sights of frothy water rapids, stands of handsome green cedars or, especially, fine gatherings of lichen-covered boulder families.

My first introduction to the Castor Shut-ins was from a friend whose family lived in Perryville. His folks had camped in pink rocks along the river for several generations. My buddy arranged numerous camping trips in the canyon, before it became a state park and overnights were finally prohibited.

Camping trips with the boys were always a hoot—literally. Owls were always there to announce our late night hikes by lantern in the woody bluffs surrounding pink rocks.

Camping trips with girlfriends were another matter entirely. Castor River Shut-ins has to be one of the most romantic locales in the Show Me State. This camper fondly recalls a late evening "show-me swim" in the pool below the shut-ins.

That swim was followed by some quality campfire time and a once-in-a-lifetime light show up in the celestial canopy. Never mind the swirl of stars twinkling above in the Milky Way; on this enchanted evening, the moon was subject to a lunar eclipse.

A full moon reflecting the pink off the Castor River rocks is a treat in itself, but to see the changing hues of the rocks as the moon withdrew was nothing short of miraculous. With the moon totally swallowed, stars and shooting stars took over the show.

Animals and noisy insects were silenced, as if awed by the unexpected loss of the moon. On a canyon horizon, lightning bolts were sparring, and low thunder rumbled in the distance.

Sorry to say, this is an experience not easily duplicated. And since state conservation took over this land donated by Ellsworth and Evelyn Amidon, late-night activities are restricted. The trade-off is that Pink Rocks is a now a protected site, a gem for you to enjoy far into the future.

MISSISSIPPI'S CHAIN OF ROCKS

THE INFAMOUS CHAIN OF ROCKS CAN BE FOUND JUST A FEW MILES DOWN-STREAM FROM WHERE THE MISSOURI RIVER POURS ITS MUDDY LOAD INTO THE MISSISSIPPI. The rock chain is a series of boulders stretching from Illinois on the east to the Missouri shore on the west.

Legends tell of past droughts when Native Americans were able to cross the Mississippi by carefully hopping from boulder to boulder. More recent tales involve human bodies emerging broken and lifeless after smashing into this stone cold demarcation line in the river above St. Louis.

The best place to observe this odd line of rocky capstones, jutting above the riverbed, is from the old Chain of Rocks Bridge. The 1.1-mile bridge is a man-made marvel, and it's perfectly suited for viewing the natural marvel of this awesome row of river teeth.

Chain of Rocks Bridge was put into service in 1929 to serve as a roadway for Route 66 between Chicago and Los Angeles. Shortly after the nearby Interstate 270 bridge opened in 1967, the Chain of Rocks Bridge closed. The old bridge seemed destined to rust and deteriorate into oblivion.

Through the efforts of hikers and bicyclists, the old bridge found new life after 32 years of dormancy. It reopened in 1999 with the new name of Route 66 Bikeway. It is still mostly referred to as Chain of Rocks Bridge.

You can stroll or ride across the high river bikeway and take in some awesome scenes looking south. Close up, there are two historic St. Louis water intake towers, which look like foreboding medieval castles protected by whirling waters. In the distance stands a giant indoor city football stadium and the towers of the St. Louis skyline.

Easily the most captivating sight for the eyes—and roar for the ears—is that rocky chain. The water coming under the bridge is swift, but flat. When it hits the rocks, it bubbles and boils, froths and foams. At some points, it seems to literally erupt from the deep, like an angry lava flow.

Today, the old Chain of Rocks Bridge is a site of joy. Families feast at picnic tables placed along its deck. Young lovers hold hands and view the sights. Kids on bikes race across the span from one state to the other.

Nevertheless, the old bridge has its darker side—and wretched secrets in its past. One of those terrible tales is told by Jeanine Cummins in her book, *A Rip in Heaven*. It's the story of a night in April 1991, when her two cousins, Julie and Robin Kelly, were assaulted, then shoved off the bridge to their deaths in the angry waters below.

Julie Kelly was a teen scribe who went to the abandoned bridge to write poetry—pleas in verse for peace and understanding. You should not shy away from visiting the Chain of Rocks because of the brutality that befell Robin and Julie; but do look to the sky when there, if only for a moment, to offer up a wish and a hope that Julie's dreams one day will be fulfilled.

In Transit at Creve Coeur Park

CREVE COEUR LAKE, LOCATED ON A FAR WEST EDGE OF ST. LOUIS COUNTY IN THE MISSOURI RIVER FLOODPLAIN, IS THE FOCAL POINT OF A SPRAWLING PARK FAVORED BY HIKERS, BIKERS, BOATERS AND ROWERS.

A good place to begin a bicycle ride is near the park's rocky waterfall, a popular site for wedding parties to have photos snapped in between the ceremony and reception. There's some irony in this local tradition, since the waterfall and park are named for a Native American maiden whose heart was broken in the pursuit of love.

The bike trail around the lake is roughly an oval, and if you begin at the waterfall in warmer months, you may be surprised at the congestion of cars, people and picnickers at this end of the park. If you choose to travel clockwise on the oval trail, you will quickly find yourself in quieter space.

As you round the southeast tip of the lake, you will begin heading west underneath the Page Avenue extension. While nature lovers objected to this highway, its deck is so high that the traffic seems far removed. Huge concrete supports seem like strange obelisks to bikers in their midst.

Soon you come to a fork, where you must choose whether to head toward the Missouri River or north on the oval around the lake. This side of the lake is heavily wooded, with blinds where you can stop to spy on the waterfowl residents of Creve Coeur.

When you reach the top of the lake, you will cross a bridge where you can see the staging area of the St. Louis Rowing Club. If the club is out on the lake, you ought to dismount from your bike to take time to enjoy the scullers.

Sculling is strenuous. All of the athletes are seated, facing backward, except for the all-important coxswain. The rowing crew must complete a course as fast as possible through the most efficient use of the oars.

Contrary to popular belief, the rower doesn't pull the oar through the water, rather the rower moves the shell past the blade of the oar which has a "grip" on the water. Each stroke accelerates the boat; the point in the stroke at which the boat is moving fastest is shortly after the oar is released from the water.

Oarsmen must preserve the boat's balance as it glides through the water. Stamina and focus are essential. Synchronicity is key. Winning races is all about technique and team work.

There is a natural beauty to the rowing club's activities on Creve Coeur Lake. Each sleek shell becomes a single living thing as all the oars hit the water—and lift up from the water—at precisely the same time.

The St. Louis Rowing Club started on the Mississippi in 1875. After disbanding in the 1950s, the club was revived at Creve Coeur in 1983. Its work is an inspiration to all the hikers, bikers, walkers and rollerbladers—everyone in transit at the park. You may even be inspired to hop on your bike for more laps around the lake.

Gem at Joplin: Grand Falls

Missourians have a strange habit of always likening the state's many natural assets to those that exist, perhaps on a grander scale, somewhere else. This is just a symptom of a wider cultural malaise: an inability to live in the here and now.

Missourians are too often disposed to compare their Mississippi River to Egypt's Nile. They refer to their geologic wonder of Grand Gulf in the southern part of the state as "Little Grand Canyon." They describe the state's largest, continuous waterfall, found south of Joplin, as a sort of "Miniature Niagara Falls."

There seems to be an implication in all of this that if you want "the real thing" you had better take a trip somewhere else. This is folly. All the natural gems in this Midwest wonderland glimmer and glow in their own right—and that is certainly the case with Grand Falls near Joplin.

Local folks like to say that on a breezy summer day you can feel a refreshing mist hit your face at Grand Falls, just like you might feel walking along the rim of Niagara Falls in New York. Perhaps. But is this comparison required to validate the experience of Grand Falls in Missouri?

Forget all this mist for a moment. Niagara Falls is full of people, traffic, noise, carbon monoxide, fast-food joints, large hotels, trinket shops, ice-cream vendors—and long lines of tourists waiting to get on some boats to feel some spray from the falls.

By contrast, Grand Falls exists as a quiet secluded wonder, surrounded by unsullied air, under an unobstructed sky. It is not junked up with honky-tonk shops, hotels, vendors or boat cruise docks.

This is not to say that Grand Falls is lifeless. The area is pocked with tiny rock pools where frogs flourish, small plants prosper and dragonflies dither. Long ago this area was under an ancient sea containing corals, sponges, strange fish, crustaceans, trilobites and the occasional shark.

The remains of these forgotten sea animals were compressed and formed into vast rock layers over eons. These layers are exposed at Grand Falls as sheets of thick chert. Shoal Creek flows over these solid shelves of chert. The waterfalls drop as much as 15 to 25 feet in a continuous liquid revelry.

Grand Falls is not a trophy spot, or a tourist snapshot; it is a place to play Siddhartha. Protagonist of Hermann Hesse's novel popular with the 1960s generation, Siddhartha is a restless youth who travels in search of varied experiences and the meaning of life.

Loosely based on the life of the original Buddha, Siddhartha comes to realize that meaning is neither an attainable objective nor a destination to be reached. He comes to this awakening beside timeless, flowing waters that speak to him of eternity.

Grand Falls can be a place for your own awakening. Listen. Ancient layers of petrified life cry out here. The waters laugh out loud. Meaning can be found here.

Gravois Creek–Grant's Trail

Useful musings on fate and human destiny need not always take place at quiet locales while you assume a lotus position. Some of the most enlightening internal discourse and progression of intellect can actually take place while in transit on a bicycle.

Thanks to the success of the rails-to-trails movement in America, bike paths are proliferating. Missouri has been a prime beneficiary of this movement. Miles of former railroad track beds have been converted into safe, abundantly scenic and accessible trails.

A favorite suburban stretch in south St. Louis County is Carondelet Greenway, renamed as Grant's Trail. The trail promises to grow in length, but the north trailhead at this writing is not too far from the pastures of the princely and exceptionally handsome Anheuser-Busch Clydesdales.

Farther down this pleasant trail, you will encounter Ulysses S. Grant's White Haven, the estate of the Busch family and Grant's Farm. You also will become acquainted with Gravois Creek. This stream is a meandering companion of the trail—sometimes hugging it closely, sometimes wandering off into weedy fields and woods.

As a partisan of President Grant, my own thoughts, while on bicycle, turn to the biography of this unappreciated and underrated leader from a period of crisis. At all times, Grant's integrity was untouched by the strife and corruption surrounding him.

He distinguished himself as a military officer both in the Mexican War and Civil War. President Lincoln saw Grant as essential to the Union cause: "I can't spare this man—he fights."

Later, as president himself, Grant fought for the rights of our country's most vulnerable—Native Americans and the newly emancipated slaves. He defied both the Ku Klux Klan as well as those intent on total extermination of America's native population. It is only now becoming apparent how different America's history might have been without Ulysses S. Grant.

As you bicycle down Grant's Trail, you will be traveling along the creek that Grant traversed from Jefferson Barracks to the home of his bride-to-be, Julia Dent. Along the way, he recited poetry and picked flowers for Julia.

According to *Ulysses S. Grant: Soldier & President,* author Geoffrey Perret says Grant once came upon a severely injured slave along the creek and bandaged him up. An impressed Julia remarked on how she thought "it was the mission of the soldier to make wounds, not to bind them up."

On one of his last trips to see Julia before military transfer, Grant almost drowned in the Gravois. Spring thaw and heavy rains sent the creek into a rage, and he was swept off his horse.

If you do choose to travel Grant's Trail—take time to smell the flowers and fathom fate. You will undoubtedly wonder how this tiny creek might have changed the fate of this big nation.

Greer Spring's Visionary

Missouri's many enchanting water sites have inspired a multitude of dreams. Some dreams have come true while those that came to naught can still stir the imagination.

Dr. Christian H. Diehl's dream was to build a sort of sanitarium or health spa at Welch Spring. Diehl's health resort, which was to be located at the north end of the Current River, would use vapors rising from the spring in Welch Spring Cavern to treat city folk with asthma and other maladies. Alas, Diehl died in 1940 before his dream was able to become a reality.

A commercial enterprise also was envisioned farther downriver at Round Spring and Round Spring caverns in the 1930s. Two businessmen from Cuba, Mo., were intent on developing the caverns into a magnet for tourists visiting the Ozarks. Although the federal park at the site now gets plenty of summer traffic, the original dream of the cavern developers fizzled.

In more recent times, St. Louis brewing giant Anheuser-Busch had designs on Greer Spring. Located by the Eleven Point River, the spring is 40 miles south of Round Spring on Hwy. 19. The brewery's dream was to use the spring, the second largest in Missouri, as a source for a great new brand of natural bottled water.

It's not surprising that the brewery was attracted to Greer Spring. The spring is formed by the convergence of three underground rivers. The ground virtually rumbles with the 222 million gallons of icy water, which flow daily into a fast-widening Eleven Point River about one mile away.

Of course, it's also not surprising that the brewery's intentions raised alarm among naturalists and environmentalists. They feared for Greer Spring's future— its fathomless depths, deep colors, endless motion and incredible force. They also worried about the spring's natural setting—cliff and crevice, rock and ravine.

With nature lovers voicing their fears that the brewery would spoil the spring property, the company backed off from its bottling plant scheme. That provided an opening for a different vision. Conservationist Leo A. Drey's dream was to acquire Greer Spring and to sell it to the U.S. Forest Service for safe public keeping.

Drey bought the natural treasure of Greer Spring in 1988 from a family that owned it for decades. It would be several years before the U.S. Forest Service could spring to complete Drey's dream. In the end, the brewery joined Drey in contributing a substantial gift so the public could acquire the 7,000-acre area at a bargain price.

Leo Drey's conservation legacy extends throughout the Ozarks and in watershed areas of the Jacks Fork, Current, Huzzah and Black rivers. But the dazzling gem of his visionary efforts has to be Greer Spring. Consider a journey to the aquamarine eye of untamed Greer Spring. It's a fine place to dream—to dream big.

HA HA TONKA SPRING

THERE IS FAR TOO MUCH CIVILIZATION AT MISSOURI'S LAKE OF THE OZARKS AND OSAGE BEACH FOR MOST NATURE LOVERS. The area's main drag, Highway 54, is packed with strip malls, fast-food joints, cheap gift shops, honky-tonk bars, country music halls and roadside attractions such as bumper cars, miniature golf and bungee jumping.

If you enter all this chaos from the north, especially in peak summer months, be ready for real bumper car action. We're talking about bumper-to-bumper car traffic, sometimes lit up at night with rotating red "bubble gum machines," as Ozark traffic cops investigate fender-bender accidents.

If you show patience and you get through all this mayhem unscathed, you will cross over the Grand Glaize Bridge. From there, within less than a half hour, you can find yourself in a bona fide natural amusement park. Ha Ha Tonka State Park is about 20 miles southwest of Osage Beach.

Ha Ha Tonka is packed with plenty of nature's own attractions. Its karst topography includes caves, sink holes, rocky chasms, porous bluffs, natural bridges and gurgling springs. Many of these features have been given names such as the Colosseum Sinkhole, the Devil's Promenade, Robber's Cave and more.

Visitors here are often seen toting cameras, lenses and video equipment in order to bring home visual booty. Ha Ha Tonka is a great place for this, because the trail walks to each of its many interesting sites are relatively short—no long hikes lugging tripods and camera gear are required.

While I have certainly yielded to the temptation to capture the sights of Ha Ha Tonka on film, slide and digital memory, my treasured images of this place are strictly mental. My favorite mental images are of Ha Ha Tonka Springs, which releases about 50 million gallons of water daily into a large, reflective blue pool.

I can close my eyes and imagine a hike to the site down the boardwalk of Spring Trail. Near the mouth of the spring, I take the image of its pool and edit characters into the scene. They are from the area's actual past. There is Daniel Boone laying out pelts in the company of Osage tribal leaders.

I can close my eyes and imagine, as well, the vistas seen from the quarter-mile Castle Trail. This trail takes you to the Ha Ha Tonka Castle ruins, but I am more interested in the views here into the gorge. I take the image of the great spring and pool below, and edit characters into the scene.

Again, my character editing follows the area's history. I picture Zebulon Pike and his small band of explorers—tiny figures on their way to discover the Ha Ha Tonka Springs.

No one can argue that the scenery at Ha Ha Tonka is most accurately captured with photographic methods. However, mental images of Ha Ha Tonka offer a totally different dimension—and are not to be compared.

JACKS FORK HIDEAWAY

MISSOURI IS CLEARLY THE QUINTESSENTIAL AMERICAN STATE. It's part Yankee, part Confederate; part Eastern pretension, part Western bravado; part Northern plain, part Southern hill country. 'Tis a jumble.

No wonder, then, that many of its best minds leave in search of something a bit more rational—a locale with a more coherent worldview.

Artist Thomas Hart Benton was one of these wandering souls. Born in Neosho, he took his palette to the U.S. capital, to Chicago, to Paris and to New York. In his prime, he returned to Missouri and mainland America—proving you can come home again.

His first work back home was the statehouse mural depicting local legends like Jesse James, Frankie and Johnny, Huck Finn and Jim. Benton's attention inevitably turned to the legendary landscape of his native region: softly rolling hills, limestone bluffs, winding creeks and rivers.

A favorite rendering of Benton's rural Missouri shows a canoeist at rest in tall grass along a meandering stream. Across the rippling water is a sand and gravel bar. Above the sandy bar is a towering bluff. Amidst all of this is Ozark flora and fauna.

What Thomas Hart Benton captured in that visual articulation is one of Missouri river country's sacred places. Interestingly enough, those places exist in myriad forms and in quantity along the flowing waters of the Jacks Fork and Current rivers.

One of those sacred places exists for me on a snaky stretch of Jacks Fork, between Alley Spring and the town of Eminence. It has all the ingredients of that Benton masterpiece, plus a cave high up the bluff.

The grassy shore area across from the river bluff is always a regular stop for the "explorers" with whom I float. After miles of dipping an oar, I seek out a solitary repose—much like Benton's lone sojourner—while the younger ones take to scaling the bluff wall to explore the prize cave.

There is magic in the youthful laughter and the brazen dares that echo along the river cliff walls. It's even more magical to listen to all this chatter while stretched out for a summer's nap in sunny river country.

There is no reason for you to experience all this vicariously through a painting or a travel book. Take action. Find your way to the Ozark Scenic Riverways. Rent a canoe. Map out a float. Listen to reason, but follow your heart. Get in the water. Just do it.

It was perfectly rational for artist Thomas Hart Benton to want to learn and emulate the art of Europe and its imitators in New York. But when he found the art of those "locales" to be too obtrusive and too synthetic, he took action.

He followed his heart—back home to river country. He got in the water. He captured scenes along its rippling length, including a lone sojourner at rest on heaven's shore. In the process, Benton created art for a homeland.

Magical Johnson's Shut-Ins

If there be one very magic locale in Missouri, where nature offers excitement for the young—and a sense of awe for their elders—that place would be Johnson's Shut-ins.

The state parks department refers to this stretch of the Black River as "Nature's Waterpark." Kids will find plenty of amusements here. Massive rocks and swift waters combine to form chutes, slides and cascades.

Potholes, full of curious underwater life, dot the rolling rock shelves of the shut-ins. Beyond the "waterpark" area are more surprises—deep, cool pools of water for wading, splashing, swimming and lollygagging.

On the drive to this state park, and later on the hike to the shut-ins area, you may be tempted to explain a little geological history of the area to the young fry you have in tow. A "shut-in" is a canyon where a river becomes confined to a narrow channel.

At Johnson's Shut-ins, the Black River flows, often noisily, over blue-gray rhyolite boulders. These huge rocks date from 1.5 billion years ago, when volcanoes threw out ash, lava and hot gases. This matter cooled to form the rhyolite, now exposed in the shut-ins area of the park.

The volcanic formations and the rock were buried under shallow inland seas for 500 million years. Later, when the sea waters receded, swirling waters went to work for millions of more years, wearing down and smoothing out the rhyolite. The exposed, canyon-like gorge of Johnson's Shut-ins is one result of that work.

Of course, explaining the shut-ins to kids is like explaining what makes a rainbow. Kids are more interested in the visible result, not the invisible mystery and mechanics of origin.

And so, when you get to the end of the trail leading to the shut-ins, don't be surprised if the kids fan off to explore and play on their own. You should warn them that the rhyolite can be slippery, as well as hard and unforgiving. Bones get broken here.

At some point, you will give up on the geology lessons and the safety advisories. The kids will be caught up in the energy of the site: sliding down rock chutes and jumping into pools.

I like to climb up top one of the tallest rocks in the canyon. There I will sit cross-legged, like a Buddha with summer sun upon my brow. More likely, I resemble some ancient babboon, surveying the mayhem of his brood in raucous play.

When the hot sun and the antics of the young get to be too much, it's time to climb back down to the water. On summer's hottest days, you will find nothing compares to submerging a weary forehead, beaded with sweat, into these rejuvenating waters.

Allow yourself to stay submerged for 10 or 20 seconds, if possible. The chaos above becomes barely audible. For a few seconds, you experience the peace of eternity among these rhyolite rocks—so old they are timeless.

Joyful Flow of Maramec Spring

Water can be a force for good or evil. Water can bring barren fields and deserts to life, but it can also be a great destroyer, bringing death and destruction to all those in its path.

Artist Thomas Hart Benton was acutely aware of the dual nature of water and depicted its varied impact on his home state of Missouri with a vibrant palette. His art is full of the joy of life along meandering streams and creeks, but his painting also captures the terror of storm and flood.

In Benton's repertoire, the artistic expression of joy and life in nature does, in fact, dominate. This is as it should be. After all, the mayhem of cloudbursts, torrents and overflowing rivers is the exception in the state. The rule is calm, smooth and gently flowing waters, as found in Missouri's many bountiful springs.

Maramec Spring, ranked among the ten largest in the state, typifies the kind of water that is a force for good. It feeds the marvelous Meramec River. Its water pours out at 100 million gallons per day.

A casual observer visiting this quiet water source would never guess the volume ushering forth from the spring. That's because the water gushes up from rocky crevices 190 feet below the surface of its pool. The pool was formed years ago when the spring channel was dammed.

Surrounding the pool is a fabulous horseshoe-like walkway. Small ponds for rearing trout border one leg of the walk. A fine Maramec Museum borders the other leg. The centerpiece of the walkway is a large grotto which sits above the pool and spring itself.

The horseshoe walkway, with the beautiful tree-covered grotto as its centerpiece, forms a sort of altar to the life-giving powers of the cold, blue water. Within the horseshoe's legs is the clear, rippling pool with easily visible trout darting this way and that.

Those healthy rainbow trout add to the sense that here is the epitome—the very best—of clean, life-giving water. These are happy trout, joyful trout. They seem to sense that they are gliding through a haven—a pristine and transparent nirvana.

Lucy Wortham James, one of the original owners of the spring, never called it nirvana. She did describe the spring site as "the most beautiful spot in Missouri." Upon her death in 1938, she authorized creation of the James Foundation to oversee the spring so that it could forever be enjoyed.

There's much to see at Maramec Spring, including the old iron mine and iron works. Iron was produced here in the 1800s, and the Maramec Museum depicts those early times.

It's best to make the pilgrimage to the altar of Maramec Spring at sunrise or late afternoon. The mystery and majesty of this water sanctuary is best experienced in a softer light. Be warned that the pool can become cloudy after a period of showers, due to runoff silt carried into the water.

MINA SAUK FALLS

THE SIGHTS AND SOUNDS OF WATERFALLS HAVE LONG BEEN A SOURCE OF CONSOLATION FOR THE WORRIED OF MIND AND THE WEARY OF HEART. A Missouri traveler can do no better than Mina Sauk Falls, near Ironton, to find such consolation.

Depending on the time of year, the source of Mina Sauk Falls can be a torrent or a trickle winding through rocky crevices along the top of Taum Sauk Mountain. At 1,772 feet, Taum Sauk is the highest peak in Missouri, and belongs to the St. Francois Mountains Natural Area.

Before reaching the point where the water cascades over a series of falls, find a rocky recline to relax upon. Stretch out and enjoy the colors of bright green pines reaching to blue skies, while anchored in volcanic rocks more than 1.5 billion years old.

If you are at Mina Sauk near dusk, you may see the shadowy figure of Mina. She will be padding along in her moccasins. If you look closely, you will see her trail is marked by tears.

Legend has it that Mina, daughter of Piankashaw Chief Sauk-ton-qua, broke a tribal taboo by secretly marrying a warrior from the rival Osage. A giant of a man, Sauk-ton-qua was outraged when he learned of his daughter's clandestine relationship. When he came upon Mina and her lover by accident near the top of Taum Sauk, he seized the young warrior and hurled him over a cliff.

Mina witnessed her newlywed's murder, and in a paroxysm of grief, she followed him in death. The beautiful teen princess leapt over the cliff. Her heartbreak among those rocks proved contagious. The rocks of Taum Sauk Mountain broke open in a crevice from which the tears of nature gushed forth over the cliff.

The violence of the Mina Sauk story was foreshadowed hundreds of millions of years ago when the mountains were first formed. A series of terrific volcanic explosions spewed dust, ash and gases into the sky. Volcanic rhyolite covered the area.

The ancient rock was later covered by shallow seas that left sand and sediment. Through the eons, nature's tears eroded away sand and sediment to reveal Taum Sauk's rocky heart.

Obviously, a sojourn to Mina Sauk Falls may soothe all those wounded in some way by love. Mina Sauk, now a spirit goddess haunting the higher elevations of the St. Francois region, may make herself available to visitors who quietly seek her counsel.

Mina Sauk roams under the heavy tree canopy of the mountain, but she also will reveal herself in nearby glades full of ashy sunflower, prairie parsley, white prairie clover, little bluestem and rattlesnake master.

Her spirit is best captured at various points along her "cascading tears" that drop more than 130 feet. Take off your shoes and socks. Rest your tired feet in the splash of Mina Sauk's tears. Rest your weary heart in the embrace of the spirit of Mina Sauk.

Roaring River Spring

In southwest Missouri, oak-hickory forests hug and smother rough Ozark ridges. Limestone outcroppings offer playgrounds for bobcats and the occasional small bear. Deep hollows boast quiet pools and sparkling springs.

The Roaring River Hills Wild Area south of Cassville is a part of all this outdoor magic. Its ruggedly handsome terrain is often tagged in state tourism brochures with the over-used description of "breathtaking."

The natural nooks and crannies of the area are indeed breathtaking, but this region of the country was breathtaking in a very different way more than a century ago. For these heavily wooded hills and valleys provided hideouts for marauders—bad men who took the last breath away from Ozark folk who crossed their paths.

These marauders, who haunted the hills, were known as Bushwhackers and Jayhawkers. They were joined by even more lawless vigilantes after the Civil War with names like the Bald Knobbers, Anti-Bald Knobbers and the Confederate Democrats.

Originally, these border-state vigilante groups were often allied with the Union or the Confederate cause. However, the causes simply became an excuse for theft, revenge killings and general mayhem. Unruly gangs of ruffians dealt in wanton destruction and senseless carnage.

Some infamous family names associated with these warring factions include the Daltons, the Starrs, the Youngers and the ornery James Gang.

Today, these family names have become part of the rough-and-tumble folklore of the region. Their transient lifestyles and escapades have been romanticized, but there is nothing actually romantic about their bloody trails and murderous ways.

Similarly, the evil deeds of the Bushwhackers and the Bald Knobbers seem to have been forgotten. Today, the names of the various vigilante groups have been taken up by sports teams, business enterprises and even entertainment groups. Perhaps this is all a way to diminish the horror of the local history; to turn past nightmares into harmless fairy tales.

Still, one way to appreciate a visit to the Roaring River Spring and the 2,400-acre state park is to remember that the bad old days in these parts really were bad. For decades, both before and after the Civil War, this region suffered banditry, physical brutality, lynchings and guerilla raids.

Some historians speculate that the geography of the area—with its forest cover, cave hideouts and deep hollows—was well-suited for crime and violence. It's a land of spider holes to hide the purveyors of dark deeds.

Alas, the Roaring River Spring is also here. It can be a source of peace and tranquility for visitors. It gushes with a cleansing water—millions of gallons of purifying water. Perhaps it's water enough to wash away the sins of this region's difficult past.

WATER WITCHES OF ROCKY FALLS

ROCKY FALLS SHUT-INS, LOCATED ABOUT NINE MILES SOUTHEAST OF THE RIVER TOWN OF EMINENCE, TAKES ON VERY DIFFERENT PERSONALITIES EACH SEASON. However, the rugged beauty of the place is not at all temporal—it's year round.

At the falls, water tumbles over shelves of multicolored igneous and sedimentary rock. An ideal time to view the water cascading down the pink rhyolite and purple porphyry is after extended spring rains, but the water source of Rock Creek always seems to offer some sort of flow.

The occasions I have had an opportunity to enjoy the rock formations and craggy cliffs of Rocky Falls have come in the heat of summer. Trickles of cool water find various channels on the rocky surface and make their way to a large, quiet pool below the shut-ins. The water then continues its frothy trek for three more miles to the Current River.

Oddly enough, it's not the primeval beauty of earth, rock and water that has captivated me on my visits to Rocky Falls. Rather, I have been overwhelmed by the skies above, full of flying, circling, swooping Valkyries.

These slender-bodied jets have a multitude of nicknames, including skeeter hawks, darning needles, mosquito hawks, devil horses and water witches. They are more commonly known as dragonflies.

Rocky Falls is a perfect home for these fascinating creatures. They live as aquatic insects in temporary water, before maturing into flying insects. And what flyers they are—with acrobatic feats performed thanks to their bright, shiny, net-veined wings.

If you are fortunate enough to witness a dragonfly air show on a visit to Rocky Falls, these cocky critters can give you a lot to ponder. They have been the object of silly superstitions and mythical madness for eons.

In our present epoch of good versus evil—you're either with us or against us—whose side are dragonflies on? Swedes once labeled them as hobgoblins bringing bad luck, while the contrary Norwegians viewed them as goddesses of love and magic.

Sit yourself down on a Rocky Falls boulder and contemplate these insect birds of the air. You may come to the conclusion that it is simply illusion to try to characterize dragonflies as either good or evil. A worthy analysis, since dragonflies also have symbolized "illusion" through the ages.

Depending on your phobias, you may feel offended when one of these pond dragons lands upon your arm or leg for a brief rest. How can they feel so confident that a big human won't crush them into insect mush with a quick slap of the hand?

Perhaps their large compound eyes and agile wings give them confidence they'll meet any challenge you might pose. And the wily dragonflies have been around for 300 million years—as long as the craggy cliffs of Rocky Falls have existed. You, after all, are only a temporary visitor.

War Clubs Echo at Round Spring

In Ozark riverways country, local folks will brag that the canoes in their part of the state far outnumber the area's actual population. Who would argue with that boast, especially after a ramble down Hwy. 19?

Highway 19 south of Salem takes you through the heart of the Ozark National Scenic Riverways. Plenty of road signs for canoe rentals dot the winding roadway. Even those signs may outnumber the local population.

Along with all the rental signs are direction signs for canoe put-ins—river access points. To get to Akers or Pulltite, you must detour west off of Hwy. 19. A great spot for a canoe put-in is farther down at Round Spring.

Round Spring contributes to the Current River with a daily water flow of 26 million gallons. The quiet spring's blue pool is deceptively still. It's hard to fathom that this water is leaving to join the nearby river.

The water emerges from a collapsed cavern at Round Spring. The cavern roof tumbled into a pile eons ago. Osage tribal folklore holds that a strong, young brave caused the roof's collapse. Angered by his companions' insults, he beat the ground with his war club until the cave-in resulted.

It's hard to imagine such violence today as canoes full of families and friends float past Round Spring from put-in points upstream at Akers Ferry or Pulltite. Many canoe trips begin at Round Spring for a peaceful 18-mile float to Twin Rivers, where the Jacks Fork flows into the Current.

Canoe trips in Missouri have not always been as peaceful as the floats that take place now on the Ozark National Scenic Riverways. In the 1960s and 1970s, angry landowners sometimes beat their war clubs like Osage braves. They took insult that canoeists were presuming rivers and streams to be public thoroughfares.

It took some time for landowners to get used to the growing presence of canoeists, and to respect the water rights of these new recruits to waterways recreation. In some instances, farmers threatened to fell timber and string barbed wire across streams to stop floaters.

In one incident on the Big Sugar River, a canoeing party was roughed up and threatened with shotguns. They were forced to break camp at night and to enter a treacherous part of the river in total darkness.

When the canoeists protested that they might capsize in the black night, one of their assailants shouted back: "I don't give a damn whether anybody drowns or not. I ought to shoot your ass." The story of the encounter made newspapers from St. Louis to Omaha.

Canoeists are generally safe from such confrontations today, particularly on rivers now under state or federal control. Still, part of the adventure of canoe trips is in the uncertainty of what encounters may be just ahead.

So hold your paddles still. Do you hear the sound of a beating war club? Do you hear angry voices ahead?

Springfield Nature Center

Once a country crossroads of sorts, Springfield, Mo., is now a convention destination. This Ozark town actually has stadiums, some shopping, a few tourist sites, a big conference hotel. . . . I mean, the place even has traffic jams!

For anyone who is not a natural for convention activities, it's also quite fortunate that Springfield does, in fact, have a nature refuge. I found it while attending a state newspaper convention during a political year.

At the convention, candidates for high office tried to outdo each other as warriors against terror, as champions of peace, as environmental protectors, as builders of highways and bridges, as responsible caretakers of our tax money. It was all so depressing.

I fled the convention for a long hike in the state nature park near the intersection of Hwys. 65 and 60. On the first portion of the hike, I could hear interstate traffic roaring south to Branson. No doubt, much of it was tourist traffic heading for those patriotic shows at the Yakov Smirnoff Theatre and Shoji Tabuchi Theatre in Missouri's entertainment mecca.

Farther down the trail, the highway noise disappeared. Soon, I found myself hiking along a swamp among grazing fawns and genuine turkeys. What a fine change of scenery from what was available back at the convention hotel—no elephants or donkeys in this Missouri backwater.

This natural oasis amidst expanding urbanism offers a little of everything, including a restored savanna, an upland forest, a bottomland forest, a narrow glade, a stream, a marsh and a portion of Springfield Lake.

When visiting the center, make sure you talk to the conservation folks about the site. They will tell you that the marsh is just "lousy" with turtles. Sounds sort of derogatory—like "infested." Take my word for it, being in a marsh that is lousy with turtles is far preferable to a convention hotel that is lousy with politicians.

The state conservation folks also will tell you that the duck blind on the lake is now a "photo blind." That means you can shoot your Kodak there, but you can't shoot anything resembling what the old cartoon hunter, Elmer Fudd, might have carried on his adventures in the woods.

On your adventure at the nature center, do consider some quality eye time in the blind. It's a great way to get close to nature, without disturbing the inhabitants. It certainly trumps the outdoor intimacy of a National Geographic wildlife special.

From the blind, you can see mink, muskrat and beaver. You can also see ducks, heron and geese. More than 160 bird species have been identified at the center. In winter, you may see an eagle snag fish from the icy waters.

But, alas, you are not likely to see any elephants or donkeys. Not even a Missouri mule. If you want that kind of political wildlife, try those fancy convention hotels in Springfield proper.

CAVES AND CAVERNS

III

KIDS AND CAVES CAN BE A SCARY COMBINATION. Mark Twain certainly knew this when he allowed Tom Sawyer and Becky Thatcher to get lost in Hannibal's underground hideout—especially with "Injun Joe" lurking below, surviving on a diet of bats.

Fortunately, contemporary kids have access to plenty of safe "show caves" now, places where they can get a different taste of the wilderness below the ground. In Missouri, many of these caves sport names like "Fantastic" and "Marvel." One of them, Meramec Caverns, even claims to be the famous refuge for the meanest outlaw of them all—it's "Jesse James Hideout," of course.

Despite all the gimmickry, the outlandish superlatives and the unabashed commercialism, these show caves are a great way to introduce youngsters to the geology, ecology and environmental issues of this unique world underground. Longtime cavers, folks who've explored hundreds of "wild caves" over the years, will tell you that far from dissing show caves most real cavers are actually grateful for the commercial caverns. These cavers are aware that show caves not only provide entertainment but also information. In recent times, that information has been focused on cave etiquette and the protection of the natural wonders under foot.

Experienced cavers know that if a parent or another relative isn't a caver, then show caves are the only way children are going to be introduced to caves and caving. Also, many show caves have "wild tours," which are guided and which have the participants carry their own lights along safe stretches. This is far superior to having children playing Tom and Becky on their own.

Missouri has more than 6,000 known caves—and counting. About three-fifths of the state is directly underlain with limestone or its cousin rock dolomite, both of which form hundreds of miles of deep, dark, wild, non-commercial caves.

Despite the plethora of wild caves, this book chooses to focus primarily on show caves, because these are the sites that readers are most likely to visit to experience the "natural wonders" underground. What's more, these are the introductions that can lead the subterranean smitten to get into the kind of caving that requires boots, gloves, helmets and three sources of dependable light.

Forget the hip boots, gloves and lighted helmets for now. There are really just four essentials required to understand and appreciate the Show Me State's great natural wonders underground. They are: curiosity, a sound mind, some environmental ethics and a new vocabulary.

Curiosity may be most important. It takes an exceptional kind of inquisitiveness to go where the sun doesn't shine—ever; to go where the small inhabitants have no sight—and no eyes; to go where the flowers are made of gypsum and the drapes are made of onyx.

A sound mind is a nice item to have before and during visits to underground wonders, especially for touring wild caves. It's important to be mindful that caving can be risky business when threatening weather could cause flooding; lighting happens to be less than dependable; clothing is insufficient for conditions that could result in hypothermia.

Environmental ethics also are more than just a frill for the responsible underground adventurer. Caves are among the most fragile environments. In most caves, broken is forever. Cavers love caves, and they work to keep caves both accessible to visitation and in as pristine a condition as possible. It's a fine line to hike, because the only way to have no impact on a cave is to never visit it at all. That's not an option for cavers.

Preventing cave vandalism and protecting cave wildlife get a lot of attention in the codes of ethics for cavers. Members of grotto clubs volunteer for cleaning up caves and sinkholes, removing cave graffiti, and adopting caves for special care in such areas as the Ozark National Scenic Riverways.

According to Missouri cavers, the real threat to the world below ground may be the bulldozer making another subdivision; the dynamiter blasting a hillside for another roadway; the developer locating rural wells or septic systems without proper regard for groundwater. Poor land use, which can contaminate and destroy natural cave features, makes littering in caves look like a minor infraction.

The degree of sensitivity to cave ethics may have a direct correlation to the level of understanding and apprehension of cave vocabulary. In order to appreciate and respect the natural beauty of caves, it's necessary to attach a name to that which is loved.

In reading about the cave selection for *Show Me . . . Natural Wonders*, you should know, at a minimum, the difference between stalagmites and stalactites. Show cave tour guides are fond of reminding visitors that the stalactite is a speleothem which hangs "tight" to the cave ceiling, while a stalagmite grips "mightily" to the cave floor.

Speleothems at Fisher Cave in Meramec State Park are among the most impressive in Missouri. A disappointment at Fisher is the number of stalagmites and stalactites broken off by tourists in the previous century. An encouraging trend this century is the work by speleothem repair teams—folks who are literally gluing pieces of cave past back together again.

Giant speleothems steal your breath away because of their massive size and the hundreds of centuries needed to make them. Soda straws, on the other hand, are thin, hollow speleothems that attract admiration for their very fragility. Soda straws at Jacob's Cave seem to gather together in dense packs for protection.

A couple of new descriptives to add to your cave vocabulary at Meramec Caverns are: satalactiflats and flowstones. Stalactiflats look like upside down mushrooms clinging to the cave ceilings in the Jungle Room. Flowstones? They're what compose the "Stage Curtains" in the theatre room at Meramec Caverns. The light shows on the flowstones at Meramec are not easily forgotten.

More incredible and unforgettable are the mineral formations found at Cathedral Cave. Stramatalites are among the world's oldest living fossils.

Stramatalites in Cathedral Cave look like small spaceships that crashed into the cave ceilings and walls. In reality, the stramatalites are giant algae buds dating from millions of years ago when the Missouri landscape was seascape—covered over by water stretching to the Gulf.

Subterranean beauties such as Talking Rocks Cavern are referred to as "living caves." They're chock full of intriguing formations that have been growing for millions and millions of years—and which continue to grow and grow.

Nature's underground mansions don't come much larger than Marvel Cave in the Branson area. Marvel boasts underground lakes and a giant waterfall more than 500 feet below the earth's surface. Marvel Cave attracts thousands of visitors every summer as part of the Silver Dollar City theme park attraction.

The natural constituency for this book may include folks who are put off by throngs of tourists and the commercialism of show caves. That's understandable.

A major part of the magic of special nature sites is to be able to get away from it all—to escape the maddening crowds in a meadow, by a brook, on a high glade.

Nevertheless, it's impossible to chronicle the natural wonders of the heartland without due attention to the splendid wilderness underground. Cave sites merit visits even if there is more foot traffic than you really want to negotiate.

Three suggestions:

• Consider touring the bathysphere canyons, buried waterworks and astonishing cavescapes during the off season. One of my favorite cave explorations was at Bridal Cave on an early October day when my guide was stuck with a single, solitary me.
• Meditate after the tour. Sites such as Meramec Caverns and Onondaga have plenty of secluded woodlands nearby. It's a joy to stretch out under an autumn sun and to think about cave scenes just witnessed. It's a wonder to think about how many autumn suns passed overhead before those mineral lily pads took shape in Onondaga.
• Get a seasoned caver to take you on a customized tour of a wild cave.

Cavers are cool people. The chance to meet and interact with cool cavers are among the rewards of writing this book. And I will always treasure my personalized tour of Cathedral Cave, where I listened to the eerie voices and the chatter of the waterfall children.

Bonne Terre Underground Mine

While Missouri may be famed as the great Cave State, not all of its subterranean expanses were cut and carved by nature's hand. The underground marvel of Bonne Terre was created, chisel stoke by chisel stoke, at the gnarly hands of lead miners.

The origins of Bonne Terre Mine can be traced back a century and a half ago, but it was hardly the first mine in the area. Mining in the Old Lead Belt of Missouri actually began almost three centuries ago on the eastern side of the St. Francois Mountains, the tallest peaks in the state.

The forgotten miners of Bonne Terre excavated its depths stone by stone, oar cart by oar cart, for 100 years from the 1860s to the 1960s. Some 30 million tons of rock and ore were removed. When the great mine finally closed, nature staked her own claim—a highly liquid claim.

Water filled the mine's depths, and nearly 100 miles of interconnected shafts, rooms and drifts went under water. The primitive workings of the mine were submerged by billions of gallons of cold, amazingly clear water.

The best way to experience Bonne Terre's "Billion Gallon Lake Resort" is in scuba-diving gear. Divers enter the Old Mule entrance of the mine for an underwater excursion between the rock-hewn columns, ballast piles, balconies, and buttresses.

If you're not into fins, wet suits and oxygen tanks, the next best way to experience Bonne Terre is as a guest of its scuba-diving enthusiasts. It was my good fortune to experience the mine on a sultry July weekend. The divers reminded me that there is no summer—no season—down in the mine. Temperatures and water conditions are consistent year-round.

Bonne Terre's scuba divers may give you a boat tour of the mine, as they gave me. Such a trip allows you to peer down into the glassy waters. There you will see the elevators, ore carts, scaffolding and great pillars wrapped in chains and cables.

Of course, it's what you will hear from the scuba gang that can be just as fascinating. They say diving the mine is like flying through the Grand Canyon like angels. They'll note that diving the mine earned a No. 10 spot on National Geographic's list of America's best adventures.

Scuba storytellers can also tell you about divers who got into trouble in these depths—stories without a happy ending. They may also tell the tale of when the mine was wired for electrical lighting, and how miners quit when they saw clearly, for the first time, how high and dangerous the catwalks were in the mine.

That story of the first watt-powered lighting in the mine provides an intriguing metaphor for life. How many of us would pull back from life's demands and challenges if we could clearly see the risks involved? Is it best that we often grope through life in a dimmer light?

Bridal Cave

No doubt about it, commercial caves can be a little on the tacky side. Guides spout cornpone humor as they narrate the tours. They will tell you that the stalactites hang "tite" to cave ceilings, while stalagmites hug the floor of a cave with all of their "mite."

Million-year-old speleothems must endure the indignity of being tagged with nicknames to amuse cavern tour ticket buyers. Geological formations often are set all aglow with garish multicolored lights.

Even tackier than what goes on underground is what goes on above ground. Highway billboards may well advertise the caves as if the portals of heaven itself await you. The cave gift shops are stocked with bags of fool's gold and cave guidebooks chock-full of questionable Indian and desperado mythology reportedly connected to the historic cavern.

And yet, all of this tackiness is, in fact, part of the charm of cave culture. It's a big part of what gets little kids interested in the nature hidden below ground—and that can't be all bad. Adults who turn up their noses at all of this cavern honky-tonk may just be suffering from a bad case of "taking everything a little too seriously."

City slickers might argue that the tackiest aspect associated with commercial caves is, in fact, a ritual—the underground marriage ceremony. In Missouri, about 2,000 couples have exchanged vows in the state's famous Bridal Cave, which rates among the top scenic caves in the country.

Bridal Cave is naturally located at 526 Bridal Cave Road. To be more specific, this wonderful cavern for wooing couples can be found beneath Thunder Mountain, two miles north of the Ozark town of Camdenton. Local folklore tells of an Osage tribal wedding ceremony held in the cave in the early 1800s.

Without getting bogged down in all of the romantic details of Irona and her love for Prince Buffalo, suffice it to say that the tale is full of love and loss, tragedy and triumph. The happy ending involves the marriage of Irona and Buffalo in the stalactite-studded hideaway that today has become the Bridal Chapel of Bridal Cave.

Should you decide to visit Bridal Cave, you'll be pleased to know that you don't have to take out a marriage license to take the tour. The cave's allure does not depend on the torrid tale of Irona and Buffalo. Massive columns, fragile soda straws and sprawling draperies adorn the cave's many rooms—not just the nook named for Native American nuptials.

As you breathe in the cool beauty of Bridal Cave, you might actually put aside any city slicker snobbery about cave nuptials. Why not declare everlasting love in a chapel formed millions of years ago? Why not wed in a temple that has withstood storms, tremors, quakes and climate change? You don't have to be a troglodyte to consider marriage in a cave.

Cathedral Cave

Blind salamanders, pickerel frogs and giant fisher spiders may startle you upon entering Cathedral Cave. As if these critters aren't creepy enough, some of the cave's tour guides suggest there are even more mysterious creatures in the cavern's midst.

These guides say they sometimes hear human-like voices from deep within the cave. The voices resemble the chatter of children and are best heard when all tours have ended and guide flashlights are extinguished.

Cathedral Cave is adjacent to the better-known Onondaga Cave and is in the same state park near the tiny town of Leasburg, southwest of St. Louis. While Onondaga is known for its many mineral lily pad formations, Cathedral Cave also can claim its own unique beauty with stramatalites.

Stramatalites? These are among the world's oldest fossils. The bulbous stramatalites in Cathedral Cave are blue-green algae buds dating from millions of years ago when Missouri terrain was covered by sea.

Cathedral's stramatalites look like meteors embedded in the floor and ceiling of the cave. They are smoothed and rounded and seem to emit a sort of orangish glow from years of interaction with mineral, mud and clay.

Stramatalites thrived as primitive life at the dawn of creation. This bit of knowledge regarding these ancient, but now lifeless, cave inhabitants may add to the creepy, crawly feelings you may feel as you travel inside this underground fairyland.

However, the stories of the human-like voices echoing in the caverns are the icing on the creepy, crawly cake. Cave guides call these eerie voices the chatter of the waterfall children.

Tours in Cathedral Cave are limited and are organized in small groups. These explorations are conducted by flashlight. One summer I enjoyed a personal tour from a guide named Anna, who told me several scary tales about the voices. Then we turned off our flashlights and listened for them.

Sure enough, waterfall children chatter soon filled the cave—and it grew in intensity the longer we kept the lights doused. The weird auditory vibrations are explained as echoes of an underwater stream's flow, but I prefer less rational explanations.

Perhaps these voices emanate from Morlocks, the strange underground inhabitants of author H. G. Wells's *The Time Machine*. In Wells's book, it's suggested that Morlocks may have devolved from humans forced to go underground after some great earthly calamity. Morlocks shun light. They live a morbid subterranean life.

If Morlocks aren't in Cathedral Cave yet, perhaps some day they will be. In the 1960s, plans were made for this cave and others in Missouri to be refuges for humans in the event of a nuclear war. And how might humans change after generations beneath the earth's surface? Would their voices sound like the waterfall children?

Contemplating Cliff Cave History

Some nature sites are deemed as "sacred" because of their dramatic aesthetics. A unique beauty instills a sense of wonderment and an inkling of eternity among mortal observers.

Other nature sites may inspire an unexpected reverence because of the human history that has unfolded over time at the location. Visitors with a mystical bent might even talk about a "psychic imprint" left behind from unusual incidents that occurred at the particular destination.

Cliff Cave along the Mississippi River, just south of the towering Jefferson Barracks Bridge, is hardly an aesthetic wonder. The entrance to the cave is in shambles and a fence is in place to inhibit exploration.

Civilization has taken its toll at Cliff Cave. Vandals have destroyed formations and the cavern walls have been defaced with spray paint. Urban pollution has deprived the cave stream of its most exotic life forms, including such former inhabitants as blind fish and albino salamanders.

And yet, Cliff Cave Park and its cavern are worth visiting. There is room to hike and to contemplate the area's active past. The cave is at the end of a wooded hollow that starts near the river and runs inland about a quarter mile to the cavern mouth.

The hollow, formed by steep hills on either side, shields the area from winds along the river. This is a sort of curse in summer but a blessing in winter when icy winds bluster. The hills on either side of the hollow must also protect the secrets of this place.

In order to appreciate Cliff Cave, it is important to bring some knowledge of those secrets as you seek to understand what the area is all about.

You should know that Cliff Cave was once known as "Indian Cave," a place where Native Americans took shelter as long ago as 7000 B.C.

You should know that Cliff Cave was a stop for French fur traders, who used the cave as a sort of tavern stop on their Mississippi River travels.

You should know that Cliff Cave was a likely haven for pirates and thieves, and later a rendezvous site for Confederates in Civil War times.

You should know that Cliff Cave has at various intervals been a storage site for spirits, both wine and beer, due to its cool temperatures and its proximity to the river.

You should know that Cliff Cave also has had a reputation as a bivouac for illegal booze during Prohibition and as a refuge for mobsters.

You should know that Cliff Cave was almost blasted shut when county police grew tired of teen parties at the site in the 1960s.

You should know that Cliff Cave is haunted by tragedy. Four boys and two adult counselors died in the cave in a flash flood during the torrential Midwest rains of 1993.

Cliff Cave is worth knowing, but not everything can be known about Cliff Cave. Its secrets are many.

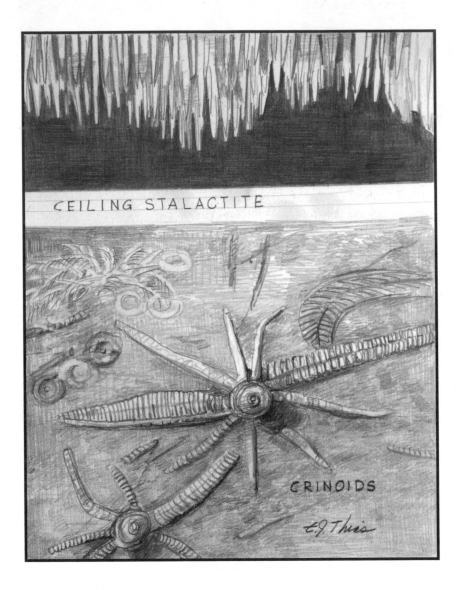

CRYSTAL CAVE'S CRINOIDS

THE FOLKS AT CRYSTAL CAVE IN SOUTHWEST MISSOURI LIKE TO BRAG ABOUT THEIR CAVERN'S PERFECT FOSSIL CRINOID CALYXES. And why not? Crinoids are a big deal. After all, these crusty ancient cretins were named as the official state fossil by the Missouri legislature in 1989.

Related to the sea urchin, sand dollar and star fish, crinoids thrived in the shallow ocean waters which covered Missouri more than 300 million years ago. Occasionally described as "sea lilies," crinoids consisted of a skeletal "flower" with a mouth, tubular stem, and five symmetrical feeding arms.

Paleontologists say crinoids filled the sea shallows, their arms rippling in the waves. These arms stretched from long and thin graceful columns. Sometimes, crinoids were preserved whole when they sank to the water's bottom and were covered with lime mud. Most of what we see today, however, are fossilized bits and pieces.

Crinoid bits and pieces are firmly embedded in the walls and ceilings of Crystal Cavern. A new cave room, opened in 2006, has a veritable mural of crinoid parts jutting from the chert walls. Thousands of the tubes, button "flowers," and arm pieces are frozen in a natural underground exhibit.

Crystal Cave's proprietors are proud of their fossils, but they don't want to just talk about crinoids. They boast that the cave is living, because the cave's soda straw stalagtites are dripping with glistening water, an indication that they are still growing.

Also of note are cavern helactites. These are collections of stalagtites which appear to have been blown sideways. Some are looped like shoe laces; others are corkscrewed like an opener for a fine bottled wine.

Crystal Cave contains a number of other notable attractions, including an underground waterfall. Also worth mention are the cavern's many glowing crystal draperies and an impressive 100-foot-tall Cathedral Room.

Despite these colossal sights, it's natural if on a visit to Crystal Cave your attention inevitably returns to the tiny crinoids. Modern-day descendants of crinoids still exist in some of our planet's oceans. The simple life forms that thrived in a sea covering Missouri are now reduced to fossils.

Haughty humans may dismiss the simple crinoids of ancient times as a small curiosity. However, consider that these crinoids in Crystal Cave were members of a species rippling their starry arms in the waters over Missouri for at least 35 million years.

By contrast, estimations of the reign of civilized man on this earth sometimes are notched at around 10,000 years. That's a pretty puny life span in comparison to the crinoids. Will we pretentious humans have the staying power of these early crinoids? How will we be preserved?

Is it too far-fetched to imagine our bones and skulls embedded in cavern walls, along with bits of crinoids, for observation by some future beings?

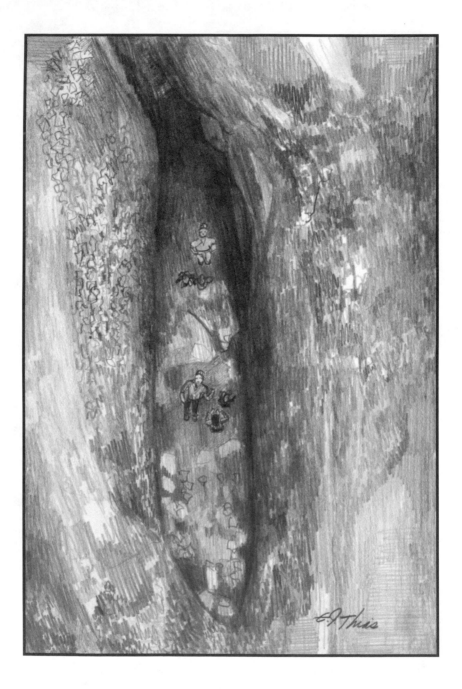

DEVIL'S ICEBOX

PEER INTO THE CRAGGY, DEEP CREVICE THAT DESCENDS INTO THE DEVIL'S ICEBOX, AND YOU MAY THINK YOU'RE PERCHED AT THE PROMONTORY OF A PIT CAVE. Pit caves open vertically. They are the delight of all would-be Indiana Jones types.

Entry into a pit cave may require reliable ropes, rappelling equipment and, above all, daring. Pit entrances sometimes bell out into wonderful underground chambers or ballrooms.

Alas, the deceptive "doorway" to Devil's Icebox is not a pit opening at all. It's actually one of two sinkholes that make up the entrance to Devil's Icebox Cave. There's a wooden staircase in the adjacent sinkhole that takes you down from the observation deck overlooking the first sinkhole.

Those stairs are part of a half-mile wooden boardwalk trail that makes Rock Bridge Memorial State Park, south of Columbia, so accessible to so many. Not everyone is elated with the replacement of deer paths and mudslick trails with the boardwalk.

The ruffians lament the loss of the area's dangerous beauty and wilderness feel. Well, they need to chill out. They will find that the Devil's Icebox Cave itself remains a very dangerous place, and a challenging exploration measured in miles.

The cave system is open only to those on Wild Cave Tours (WCT) that are park-led by experienced cavers. Tours are graded at four levels, with the most strenuous requiring wading, stooping, clambering and crawling.

According to the Department of Natural Resources, possible hazards on a WCT include: bruising falls, cuts, lacerations, hypothermia, canoe capsizing, rescue delays and drowning.

If you can overlook the potential hazards on a WCT, you may be rewarded with visits to such delightfully named underground features as the snowbank, waterfall, bat room, belfry, wormhole, dripstone cascade, boxwork heights, brachiopod room, rollercoaster, hollow dome and more.

Make no mistake, however, the icebox is nothing to mess with. People have died here, including two men in their 20s whose canoe flipped inside the cave depths. Give the devil his due. Keep in mind, this place is used for emergency cave rescue practices.

If you can't overlook the potential hazards of a WCT, that's okay. Visit anyway. Visit Old Beelzebub's sinkholes, and take a look from top and bottom. After gazing up the moss-covered slash to inviting blue skies, gaze into the cave's netherworld.

As a moral relativist, I have always felt quite comfortable at the Devil's Icebox. As a climatological relativist, I have always marveled at how cool and refreshing this place can be in summer; while in winter, it's a damp refuge from the frigid winds blowing above the slippery sinkholes of Satan.

Devil's Icebox is appropriately named. It's a temptation to tour. However, it should be left to the bats and blind water creatures as a place to call home.

Fantastic Caverns, Fantastic Ride

Folks full of environmental sense and sensibility may be put off by all the publicity, pomp and hype used to draw visitors to Fantastic Caverns, an underground attraction just north of Springfield in the Missouri Ozarks.

Fantastic's front men bill it as one of the few caves in the world large enough to maneuver a motor vehicle through. They tout Fantastic's Jeep-drawn trams which transport happy sightseers on a mile-long, 50-minute tour. The implicit message: no walking necessary here to enjoy the subterranean scenery.

All of this may seem to be apostasy from an environmental standpoint until you learn that the Jeeps used in the caves are fueled by propane. They emit only oxygen and water vapor. What's more, the owners of the cave are involved in protecting the cave wildlife, monitoring pollution and opening the cave to schools for environmental education purposes.

The tram rides may give this nature experience too much of a Disneyworld feel, but after all, they do make it possible for grandparents and youngsters to make an underground visit that might otherwise be entirely too strenuous. Consider, also, that the trams only touch the cave floor with eight wheels on each tour, as opposed to the impact of hundreds of human feet.

So, please, put all the environmental reservations aside and just enjoy the Fantastic ride. It's a crystalline journey full of stalactites hugging the ceiling and stalagmites growing from the floor. Glistening rock pillars seem to be decorated in thickening icicles of rich vanilla ice cream.

Fantastic Caverns, with its glowing cave pearls and shimmering rimrock, gives the appearance of a sort of fairyland. It came as something of a shock to learn that this magical place has been a site of evil and misery.

An old-timer on a tram trip with me provided stories that were not part of the regular tour narrative. He told several tales of Native American Cherokees taking refuge in the cave from their long, forced march to exile in Oklahoma. He also pointed to cave passageways where he suggested the Ku Klux Klan once set up shop.

If a few wanderers on the forced march of the Trail of Tears were once able to find solace in these depths, well, that is not entirely bad. You wonder if the eternal calm of these caverns afforded, at least, some temporary calm for the reluctant travelers.

It is not so easy to reconcile the past presence of the Ku Klux Klan in this beautiful place. How could hate find a home here? Decades before the cave became a tourist attraction, the Klan would hold its council meetings here, before emerging in sheets and hoods intent on dastardly deeds.

It is so very wretched, but perhaps there is something natural about hate finding its headquarters in a place where the light of day never shines.

Healing Nature at Fisher Cave

Caves of the Meramec River Valley were once prime party caves. Parties would consist of a gaggle of good old boys drinking corn whiskey, or they might involve the local society types who'd fill a cavern with quality food, drink and band music for dancing.

Meramec Caverns was the site of huge summer dances held under the glow of wall torches, before the availability of electricity. River-area historians tell tales of a state inaugural ball in Fisher Cave organized in 1865 by an enterprising governor of Missouri named Thomas C. Fletcher.

Cave parties were a mixed bag. On the plus side, the cavern acoustics for music and the underground scenery made celebrations unique. Imagine a dance held a third of a mile down inside a cave amidst towering stalagmites and onyx dripstone curtains.

On the minus side, caves could be clammy, muddy and puddly. Wooden plank dance floors offered some limited protection, but the emphasis is on the word "limited." To make matters worse, add to this climate made for mushrooms all the smoke from lanterns necessary for lighting. The trapped haze and fumes eventually drove the party animals out for air.

Of course, the human revelry was not exactly the best thing to happen to caves either. Smoke and foot traffic damaged cave ecology. Kilroys wrote their names on cave walls and some of those signatures remain 100 years later. Stalagmites and fragile soda straw speleothems were broken; some carried off as souvenirs.

At Fisher Cave, parties were called to a halt in 1926 and a padlock placed on the entrance gate. Decades later, this Meramec cave reopened for more responsible visitors and for educational tours. Much of the damage of the past can never be undone. Cave naturalists are, however, taking steps to undo some of the past destruction to wonders such as Fisher Cave.

So, how do you repair a one-of-a-kind stalagmite that took hundreds of thousands of years of mineral-laced, cavern-ceiling drips to form?

Speleothem repair teams will tell you that the first thing you have to do is find the broken pieces. Finding the severed sickles in a cave's darkness, and then matching the pieces to their stumps, can be tougher than finding that virtual needle in a haystack.

When correct matches are made, cave floor stumps and their prodigal pieces must be thoroughly cleaned. Then, an adhesive is used to put the special cavern humpty-dumpties back together again. A speleological expert who works with 3-M glues in Springfield is credited with selecting the perfect glue for stalagmite reunions.

Obviously, only a fraction of the speleothems damaged in the past can be repaired today. Nevertheless, it is always better to light one candle than to curse the darkness. And in this matter of cave rehab, it is better to repair one stalagmite than to harp upon the mistakes of an earlier time.

Graham Cave

For a mid-travel respite from the roar of traffic between St. Louis and Kansas City on I-70, consider a stop at Graham Cave. Just east of the banks of the Loutre River, Graham Cave is more grotto than cavern.

The Graham family bought the nearby Loutre River bottomland from Daniel Boone's son in 1816 and eventually purchased the property housing the cave itself. The Graham farm used the cave to shelter hogs, and then, in 1930, allowed University of Missouri professors access to consider its archeological potential.

Archeological studies since 1930 have produced astonishing revelations. Native Americans have used the cave at various times throughout the past 10,000 years. Hunters and fishermen used the cave initially and left weapon artifacts behind.

Studies conclude that these early dwellers occupied the cave on a seasonal basis and used it as a locale to consult with the supernatural. A ring of rocks surrounding a huge stone, speculated to be a council ring for ceremonial use, was found in the cave.

A visitor today should consider sitting just below the grotto's archlike entrance, which spans 120 feet wide and is more than 16 feet high. Imagine sparks adrift from a small ceremonial fire, the slow rhythm of a drum beat, and the soothing repetition of ancient incantations celebrating the bounty of the earth and its streams.

The wisdom of this grotto shelter is the wisdom of modesty, moderation and humility before the gifts of nature which provide us life.

The intact grotto, Graham Cave, stands in stark contrast to a famous grotto deep in the Shawnee National Forest of Southern Illinois. The grotto in Illinois was once far more magnificent than the one nestled in the hills of central Missouri. But much of the roof of the Shawnee grotto has collapsed into a tangle of boulders.

The inhabitants of the Shawnee grotto engaged in wild and noisy celebrations of their hunting prowess. They were an ego-mad lot. Once, more than 200 warriors built a tremendous ceremonial fire with flames licking the roof of the grotto.

The warriors were more interested in creating a spectacle than imparting any heartfelt message of thanks to earth's spiritual forces. The fire's flames eventually split the grotto roof, killing all of those below. An errant member of the tribe returned from a journey several days after the calamity only to find bits of cracked skull and bone amidst the boulders. Blood seemed to ooze from the grotto floor.

The Shawnee grotto provides a terrifying lesson on the pitfalls of excess masquerading as worship. Graham Cave's grotto speaks to us of temperance and restraint. Those who allow the grotto's spirit to enter them, while visiting Graham Cave, may well overcome the temptations of ostentation and the trap of grand gestures and pointless pursuits.

PREHISTORIC JACOB'S CAVE

FOR SALE: CAVE DATING BACK TO THE GASCONADE DOLOMITE ERA ABOUT 42 MILLION YEARS AGO. Cave has survived ice ages as well as three epic upheavals, including the 1811–12 New Madrid earthquake. Make best offer. Leasing arrangements also considered.

At the time of the writing of this profile of Jacob's Cave, the cavern in west central Missouri was actually up for sale. It seems a bit odd having such a natural wonder up for sale. It's like putting a piece of blue sky on the auction block or a fine parcel of ocean up for purchase in the miscellaneous section of a newspaper's classifieds.

Of course, most caves are in private hands and can be bought and sold. A smaller portion of these subterranean spectacles are part of the state park system. Caves found in Mark Twain National Forest get some federal protection, but most caves in Missouri are private property. About 25 show caves cater to tourists in the state.

With more than 6,000 known caves in Missouri, it would be impractical to have all these underground sites in the public domain. Fortunately, many state landowners are becoming more sensitive to their responsibilities in caring for these subsurface domains.

As a privately owned subsurface wonder, Jacob's Cave was first opened to tourists as a show cave in the Lake of the Ozarks area in 1932. Obviously, Jacob's Cave had plenty of history before its opening as a commercial cave in the Depression Era.

The folks at Jacob's Cave will tell you the cave was discovered by a lead miner, Jacob Craycraft, about 1875. Craycraft was disappointed with the minerals found in the cave, but he did, at one point, give lantern-lit tours for $.25 admission.

In the late 1940s, the cave was outfitted to be a genuine show cave with improved access, user-friendly trails and inside lighting. Tourists on Hwy. 5 were greeted by a neon sign as late as midnight. Much has changed since that sign blazed, but Jacob's Cave remains a top state show cave.

If you go to Jacob's Cave, you will be introduced to its "recent history" by guides on a mile-long tour. However, it's the ancient history that is mind-boggling. Owners advertise the cave as "almost older than history itself."

In the time before humans found a place on the planet, geologists say the cave was rocked by prehistoric earthquakes—far more powerful than the famed 1812 New Madrid calamity. One such upheaval, about 16 million years ago, took down tons and tons of giant mineral ceiling formations.

Imagine this scene in prehistory: The cave's reflective pools begin to shimmer and swell. Millions of soda straw stalactites angrily rattle together before shattering from the ceiling. Finally, giant geodes join the fragile crystals in crashing to the heaving floor of Jacob's Cave.

Cave for sale or lease: Generally safe, except in times of epic upheaval.

Mark Twain Cave

A boy's paradise—of what would that consist? Well, according to Mark Twain, there must be a river to swim in, a forest to get lost in, and certainly a cave in which to explore.

All of these essentials for a boy's paradise were a part of young Samuel Clemens' Hannibal, Mo. The young boy, who would later become America's premiere author as Mark Twain, thrived with his rascal friends in the "boy's paradise" of Hannibal.

The river was an unpredictable Mississippi; the forest was the rolling woods of midland North America; the cavern was a limestone maze—millions of years old—McDowell's Cave. They made up the playground and the inspiration for Twain's stories of Huckleberry Finn and Tom Sawyer and little Becky Thatcher.

In young Samuel's time, the cave was occasionally home to the derelict "Injun Joe," who once got lost in the underground maze and survived on a diet of bats. It also was home to the encapsulated corpse of a 14-year-old girl, placed there as an experiment in petrification by a St. Louis medical college.

Today, the frightening Injun Joe and the petrified corpse are gone. The cave itself is now named for Twain. Visitors are led on tours that pose little challenge—walkways are level, smooth, and there are no steps. Unlike many other Missouri caves, there is no mud or dripping or puddling on this tour.

You could say Mark Twain Cave is child's play. And that, after all, is its charm. Never mind the memorized routine of the tour guide, as "fantastic formations" such as Grand Avenue, Alladin's Palace and the Alligator are highlighted. Think, instead, of this young Twain fellow, and his coterie, exploring the cave and having a ball.

"By and by somebody shouted, 'Who's ready for the cave?' Everybody was," wrote Twain in his tales of Tom Sawyer. "Bundles of candles were procured and straightaway there was a general scamper up the hill."

How much has been lost for today's youth in a world of multiplying subdivision developments and strip malls? While natural spaces shrink, so, too, has the time for youngsters to engage in the childhood rites of serendipity.

To capture a lost past, there now are Environmental Literacy Summits to find ways to introduce children to nature and to allow their young imaginations to blossom. Alas, youthful nature experiences are now classified by child experts as "vicarious," "structured" and "spontaneous."

A new Twain might take to satirizing such lingo or the attempts to bring kids back to nature with Cave Crawls, Owl Prowls and Insect Safaris. But these efforts shouldn't be dismissed, nor "nature summitry" discouraged.

Also, consider Twain's Cave for a reunion of child and nature. You should go—in search of those truly free spirits of Huck, Tom and Becky.

Marvel Cave

Most tourists come to Branson for what's above ground. Water parks, wax museums, miniature golf, go-cart tracks, shopping strips—and the celebrity theaters of Bobby Vinton, Andy Williams, Jim Stafford, Yakov Smirnov, Tony Orlando . . .

More crowd-stoppers above ground include the sprawling Ozark-themed amusement park heralded as Silver Dollar City. Once a model, old-time village with a collection of craftspeople, the park is now packed with high-tech thrill rides sporting names like Lost River, BuzzSaw Falls, Fire-in-the-Hole and Thunderation.

Ironically, it was a famous natural attraction below ground, known as Marvel Cave, which began drawing throngs of tourists to the area after World War II. The cave has long since been overshadowed, if not quite overwhelmed, by the glitz and gimmickry of the new man-made Branson.

Located within the perimeter of sprawling Silver Dollar City, Marvel Cave is not your ordinary show cave. Visitors to Branson and the theme park should take advantage of the opportunity to tour the deepest cave in Missouri. The cave boasts two underground lakes and a waterfall more than 500 feet below the surface.

Visitors are often most impressed by the huge Cathedral Room, which has hosted concerts, hoedowns, weddings—even a hot air balloon. The cave also sports geological formations appropriately titled Liberty Bell, the Sphinx and Arrowhead Entrance.

The cave, which is actually located a few miles west of Branson, has had many names since its discovery by Native Americans, reportedly in the 1500s. The Osage tribesmen called it the Devil's Cave. They told of strange screeching noises spiraling up from the cave's depths—aural evidence for the presence of evil spirits.

Explorers later arrived at the deep cavern in southwest Missouri with hopes that it would produce gold and quality marble. It became the "Marble Cave," but the treasures sought never actually materialized. It was opened in the late 1800s as a tourist attraction, where visitors could marvel at its vastness, hence, "Marvel Cave."

Dedicated cavers, speleologists and spelunkers sometimes dismiss show caves as commercial monstrosities. Marvel Cave, however, gets singled out as a well-maintained beauty that provides a marvelous underground experience for thousands of people. For youngsters, Marvel Cave may well inspire a life-long interest in the wilderness underground.

If you introduce your youngsters to Marvel, be sure to retell the old Osage stories of strange noises emanating from what was the "Devil's Cave." Oh, yes, and don't take them into the cold cave when they are still drenched from all the Silver Dollar City water rides. The strange noises in Marvel should not include the chattering of the tiny teeth of shivering children.

MERAMEC CAVERNS

WHEN JOE WOOD MOVED UP FROM BEING A MERE COPY BOY TO THE EXALTED POSITION OF PHOTOGRAPHER AT THE OLD *St. Louis Globe-Democrat*, THE KID FROM KIRKWOOD, MO., GOT THE IDEA OF TAKING PICTURES OF ONE OF MISSOURI'S GREATEST NATURAL ASSETS—CAVES.

The year was 1935, and the paper had just acquired some new flashbulb equipment. Wood asked his editor if he could try this new-fangled technology on a trip to cave country along the Meramec River. He got the nod.

Some miles down Route 66, Wood spied a cardboard sign that declared: "Meramec Caverns This Way." Wood followed the signs down a rugged dirt road until he met up with Lester Dill and Pete Peterson, two caveologists who were covered with mud.

The duo invited Wood to document their latest discovery in the cavern. Wood donned overalls, then he descended on hands and knees down a shaft. He pushed a four-by-five speed graphic camera, a wooden tripod and 150 pounds of camera baggage in front of him.

Wood took the very first pictures of the Stage Curtain Room at Meramec Caverns. The curtains are made of a towering collection of stalactites, stalagmites, onyx drapery, flowstones and layers of dripstone. The curtains became part of the first photogravure layout of the caverns for the *Globe*.

Today, the Stage Curtain Room is the final stop on cavern tours that include such sites as the underground river, a Jungle Room festooned with speleothems, an Echo Room, an Onyx Mountain and a Wine Room covered with knobby clusters of rocky grapes.

Wood's photographic work at the caverns did not end with the historic shots of the flowstone curtain room. In 1948, he was called back by Lester Dill to help document and confirm the return of a century-old Jesse James.

History has it that the James Gang used the cave in the 1870s as a hideout after bank heists and train robberies. James was supposedly shot and killed in 1882. However, in 1948, a man who claimed to be the original Jesse James surfaced in Oklahoma.

He was brought back "home" to Meramec Caverns, where Woods met up with him in an investigation of his authenticity. In the three years before the ornery man's death at 104, Wood followed up numerous leads and came to the conclusion that here, indeed, was the real Jesse James.

Wood has passed on, but he left a testament, *My Jesse James Story*, which makes a case that the old man was the genuine article. A favorite Wood photo shows the bed-ridden outlaw at the cave flanked by two survivors of his Quantrill's Raiders.

Nature's million-year-old, water-sculpted rock formations will wow most adult visitors to these caverns. For younger visitors, it may take the tales of Jesse James to capture their imaginations. In either case, there's more than enough rock—and legend—for all who enter Meramec Caverns.

Onondaga's Underground Oracles

Lily pads that polka-dot marshy wetlands of America's rivers provide a transient beauty. These vibrant green islands fade and finally crumble into a brown dust and sink into oblivion.

The famous lily pads thriving in the 400-million-year-old Onondaga Cave present a beauty that is seemingly eternal. These curious formations are found in the cave's Lily Pad Rooms. Formed by cave minerals clamming onto partially submerged stalagmites over eons of time, these flowers have attracted the multitudes every year to Onondaga.

Natural inspiration can be found in the subterranean world of Onondaga, but you may have plenty of company while seeking the muse. Onondaga has been a tourist site since the 1904 St. Louis World's Fair, when it came into its own as a visitor destination.

The cave's name, "Onondaga," has more to do with crass commercialism than any Native American wisdom. Those seeking to unlock cavern mysteries by dissecting the strange-sounding "Onondaga" will be sadly disappointed. The cave's name, which means, "Spirit of the Mountains," was hijacked from the eastern Iroquois.

There are no real mountains near Onondaga and even fewer Iroquois. The name for this magnificent cavern originated with a name-the-cave contest in 1904.

Onondaga is just an hour out of St. Louis at Interstate 44's Leasburg exit. If you can get past the tourism and the company of other visitors, the deeps of Onondaga can affirm the poets: truth is beauty, beauty is truth.

Nature has provided the clearest lesson with Onondaga: there can be beauty below the surface—at levels normally beneath our conscious awareness. This is the great spiritual wisdom of Onondaga. The beauty of the world above Onondaga is perpetually in transition—lost and found, and lost again—while the beauty below is simply perpetual.

Lessons do not just flow from the million-year-old lily pad stalagmites at Onondaga. Other sages find home here. The stalactites, flowstones, rimstone dams, draperies, soda straws and cave coral are all rock-of-ages oracles in Onondaga's deep interior.

In Onondaga's Cathedral Hall, you can experience the beautiful musical tones that are vibrations of certain stalagmites. They provide the live musical notation of what some would call the Earth Mother.

Can it really be that an Earth Mother breathes at Onondaga? Well, consider that she does exhale cold air through her mouth all summer; and she inhales warm air all winter.

Onondaga offers proof for those living earth theorists, who speak of earth's life force as Gaia. The planet itself is a living, breathing organism. The breath of Onondaga gives life to its stone lily pads, and it gives hope to those who wish to know a beauty that is less obvious and less fleeting.

Ozark Cave's Miracle Mist

For those inclined to believe in winged creatures of the supernatural variety, there are good angels and bad angels. Good angels range from that great messenger known as Gabriel to a heroic warrior named Michael.

Lucifer is the most notorious bad, fallen angel. Often likened to Satan himself, wily Lucifer was reportedly thrown out of heaven for the sin of insolence and pride. He was exiled to an absolutely dreadful netherworld domain, where the old devil plots his revenge as an adversary of mankind to this day.

In Missouri, you probably can't get much closer to Lucifer's netherworld domain than by exploring an unlit Ozark Cave. Early settlers of the area must have wondered whether they would confront the conniving Lucifer on their underground forays into a totally unchartered darkness.

Based on the historical accounts of early caving, the evil Lucifer never actually materialized in the channels below ground. However, some cavers apparently did sense the presence of guardian angels. Guardian angels are a special class of ministering angels who protect and guide the hapless earthlings to whom they are assigned.

At Ozark Caverns, just east of the Lake of the Ozarks, irrefutable evidence exists that guardian angels are alive and well in Missouri. An angelic manifestation is found in the cavern's incomparable visual phenomenon accurately described as the "Angel's Shower."

The shower seems to miraculously emerge from solid rock. The streams of crystalline fluid descend among some of the most beautiful geologic wonders to be found in any sacred subsurface site. Geologists point to the Angel's Shower as the clearest indication that Ozark Caverns is still alive—it's an active cave where seeping, dripping, bouncing water drops are inspiring new formations, from stalagmites to great bunches of soda straws.

How appropriate that the mark of the angel of goodness in Missouri is a sparkling, misty shower of water that never ends. In contrast with many other states, Missouri is blessed with lakes, springs, streams, rivers and, of course, a confluence of the continent's two major water sources: the mighty Mississippi and the wide Missouri.

These water sources are just the ones that we can see. Then, there are those many flows of water below the surface, invisible like angels, but occasionally making an appearance at blessed sites such as Angel's Shower.

So, where is Lucifer in all of this, you may ask? If there are good and bad angels, where do we see Lucifer's handiwork? The best guess is that old Beelzebub's hot breath is felt upon the land in the depths of August, when intense heat and drought reduce all vegetation into a crumbly mass of brown.

At these times, it is best to consult with your guardian angel. Her shower at Ozark Caverns can reassure you, for she always flows—even in the worst of hellish heat and devil's drought.

RIVER CAVE

A PATHFINDER IS AN INTREPID SOUL WHO BLAZES TRAILS THROUGH PREVIOUSLY UNEXPLORED REGIONS. Count the brave frontiersman Daniel Boone as one of this nation's premier pathfinders.

Boone is often credited with the exploration and settlement of the great state of Kentucky. Few know that he spent almost the last quarter century of his life in Missouri, where he continued to pursue an explorer's life until his death at age 85.

At 66, Boone started a new life in Missouri. He and his son, Nathan, built a sturdy family home of timber and quarried limestone near Defiance up the Femme Osage River. Most folks, at 66 years, would be content to stay put in such a home, but Boone chose to use his mansion as a base to explore areas west of the Mississippi.

Inevitably, Boone came upon the marvelous "karst" wonderland that is today's Ha Ha Tonka State Park. Karst topography provides a magical landscape packed with sinkholes, caves and natural bridges. Streams flow underground here, while bubbly springs percolate above ground.

Ha Ha Tonka is miles to the west of Boone's home, but distance was no factor for a seasoned pathfinder. The rangers at today's Ha Ha Tonka State Park will tell you that Daniel Boone was just as at home in this wilderness full of karst formations as he was back at the mansion near Defiance.

Boone was no stranger to setting up camp for extended periods in the caves of Kentucky. He enjoyed similar lodging at Ha Ha Tonka in Missouri.

Among the caves at Ha Ha Tonka are Devil's Kitchen, Robbers' Cave, Counterfeiters' Cave and River Cave. Located at the bottom of a sinkhole, River Cave can be explored by agile humans for 700 feet and contains a giant column stalagmite. In winter, large ice teeth form near its entrance to ward off the wary and the timid.

Boone would not be intimidated by cavern ice teeth. Stories abound that Boone used River Cave and other underground hideouts to stash pelts on winter hunts. He hid the pelts from the marauding Osage, until he was ready to head back home to the St. Louis area with his prize furs.

Ha Ha Tonka was a favored retreat for Boone, and it remains a natural playground. If you wish to attempt to retrace his steps, plan to spend a day here. No doubt, Boone was familiar with the Colosseum Trail area, which winds through a massive natural bridge. Trails can also get you to River Cave and the Devil's Kitchen.

While you may not be a pathfinder in the tradition of Daniel Boone, Ha Ha Tonka is the perfect retreat for any spiritual pathfinder. Grab a park map and seek out a quiet place to sort through life's confusion.

"I have never been lost, but I will admit to being confused," Boone once remarked. Taking a short timeout to confront your confusion is a sure way to avoid being permanently lost.

Rock Bridge

IF YOU'RE AN OUTDOORS ENTHUSIAST WITH A FIRM BELIEF IN THE PHYSICAL AND PSYCHIC BENEFITS OF CONSORTING WITH NATURE, THEN IT'S ONLY NATURAL THAT YOU WOULD WANT TO SHARE YOUR PASSION.

Alas, the people you care about the most may not be so interested in sharing your passion. They may roll their eyes at the idea of a long trek in the woods or an underground adventure with some of your spelunking friends.

In such circumstances, the key to making new nature converts is to ease the neophytes into your earthly endeavors. A fantastic site for conversions of the reluctant is Rock Bridge State Park in the middle of Missouri.

My first acquaintance with Rock Bridge was as a graduate student at the nearby university in Columbia. If I remember correctly, many students of experience shared their passion for nature with novices at Rock Bridge. Much learning has taken place here.

First referred to as "Pierpont" by French settlers, Rock Bridge has a little bit of everything in one compact location. Easily accessed trails wander through forests, glades and grasslands, as well as along streams, sinkholes, ponds and fern-lined cliffs.

Of course, the highlight of Rock Bridge is the bridge of rock, which is actually an abbreviated tunnel. This karst tunnel was once part of a cave system. When a portion of the cave roof collapsed, the tunnel became an isolated, natural feature unto itself.

Hence, Rock Bridge is a cave that's not a cave. For that reason, it's just a perfect place to introduce the hesitant to the absolute wonders of openings in the earth. There are more than 6,000 known openings in Missouri that actually qualify as caves.

Rock Bridge is 150 feet long, up to 75 feet wide, with a 15-foot ceiling. A boardwalk traverses it, so boots aren't essential despite a stream that runs through it. Neither does Rock Bridge require safety helmets, headlamps, flashlights or any cave equipment.

Ghosts of the past inhabit Rock Bridge, but there's no need to mention this to any newcomer that you bring along with you. You can explain that the bridge area was once home to a mill in the 1820s, a blacksmith shop, a general store and, later in the century, a whiskey distillery. A terrible fire put an end to its rye production in 1889.

It's so hard to believe Rock Bridge was once a commercial site for country folk to congregate. In early spring or late fall, it's possible for you and a newcomer to even find solitude here. Consider a hike to the darkest portion of the "cave." Sit a spell on the boardwalk; watch your steamy breath disappear; treat your ears to the soothing trickle of the cave stream.

The beauty of Rock Bridge is that it's a place "to get your feet wet"—in a cave that's not a cave—without actually getting your feet wet. And if your newcomer friend likes it, you just might hike farther up the boardwalk to the Devil's Ice Box Cave. Now, that's a real cave.

Round Spring Caverns

When cavers rave about "heavily decorated passageways," they're not talking about the artistic touches of a crazed interior decorator of the underground; nor are they referring to the graffiti defacing unprotected caves.

A cave with heavily decorated passageways is a motherlode of gem-like formations—rimstones, dripstones, flowstones and more. A cave such as Round Spring Caverns along the Current River easily rates among the most heavily decorated in Missouri.

The main passageway of Round Spring Caverns has a high ceiling and porous walls adorned with red clay deposits. The cave is famed for its Tobacco Room, so named for its large reddish-brown stalactites that hang like bunches of drying tobacco leaves.

Over the eons, the talented interior decorators for Round Spring Caverns have consisted of water, gravel and sediment. Sedimentation gives a cave both texture and color. The sediments that invaded Round Spring Caverns were full of silt, sand and a sticky red clay, which adhered to everything.

These sediments packed the cave for many years, until torrents of water chased most of the gummy debris out. A rich, red paint job of clay, pigmented with iron oxides, is part and parcel of what has been left behind.

Trained park rangers, who provide regular guided tours of Round Spring Caverns, offer a "sedimental journey" into the cave—with explanations of the ins and outs of its clay coloration. They may also offer a warning to avoid contact with the cave's damp clay—the paint's not dry yet—and the iron oxides can stain clothing.

Local history has it that two men from Cuba, Mo., got plenty stained with red cavern clay in about 1931. They were looking to start a commercial cave— a heavily decorated cave, such as this beauty at Round Spring. It fit the bill. It operated as a show cave for years, but today the subterranean tours have a more educational bent, thanks to the rangers.

In this enlightened era—when Indians are Native Americans and history is politically correct—it may just be time to revise many anecdotal tales of the Ozark turf. For example, did two show cavers from Cuba really "discover" Round Spring Caverns?

Anthropologists will tell you that Ozark caves were probably first "discovered" and occupied by Native Americans, sometime between 10,000 and 8000 B.C. Native peoples found refuge from weather and insects in the open caves.

Round Spring Caverns would have also provided early Ozark inhabitants with clay for pottery and pigments for body paint—perhaps the colors for a ceremonial dance or a war party.

Should you visit the caverns and find yourself accidentally "painted" with red clay stains, do not curse your fate. Instead, consider yelling out a hearty war whoop to celebrate your "sedimental journey" of discovery.

Talking Rocks Cavern

Some of my New Age friends argue that the earth is a living being. They say the earth is a rich amalgamation of animate and inanimate forms that comprise an interconnected, but unitary and organic consciousness.

Who am I to argue with that? I would rather listen than argue. The New Agers refer to the living earth as "Gaia," after the so-named Greek Earth Goddess. According to their thinking, Gaia is a universal energy and life force present in all natural things and everywhere on earth.

It's easy to conceive of this Gaia being present in a forest full of night chatter or in a gurgling stream teeming with underwater creatures. It's not so easy to imagine Gaia's presence in the karst and chert of cold caves, starved of even a ray of sunlight.

And, yet, this earth spirit is most certainly present in a place like Talking Rocks Cavern. For this odd cavern is a "living cave"; it's full of intriguing formations which have been growing for millions and millions of years—and which continue to grow.

Talking Rocks Cavern, west of Branson, is one of many underground wonders found on the vast Springfield Plateau in southwest Missouri. Most of these caves are "alive" because they show the telltale signs of past Native American dwellers; they are home to teensy creatures that have adapted to the darkness; they are full of great gardens of exotic crystalline life.

Talking Rocks Cavern boasts more than 90 formations, including an overwhelming 18-foot stalactite dripstone. Even more impressive than its size is the thought of nature patiently bringing this denizen of the darkness to life with uncountable years of tiny water droplets acting upon minerals.

Another sure sign of rock life in the cavern—and of Gaia—is in its many deposits of onyx. Some New Agers and crystal healers believe that onyx gives off vital earth energies. These calm fears and worries while bolstering strength and stamina.

In the main, Talking Rocks consists of a huge chamber more than 100 feet high and 250 feet long. It's an underground cathedral hung with massive crystal draperies. You half expect these weighty Gargantua, these gargantuan growths, to break loose and crash upon the cathedral floor into a million shattered pieces.

Gargantua was a giant king noted for his enormous physical and intellectual appetites. At Talking Rocks Cavern, you sense the magic of Gaia breathing life into the formations that adorn this dark fairyland. However, you actually witness with your own eyes the power of Gargantua.

You see the outstretched arms and rocky hands holding onto the walls and ceilings. You pray that these grips won't be lost, at least, not as long as you traverse the walks, stairs and cavern platforms. Be grateful you're safe in the presence of onyx, soother of fears, provider of strength.

Vineyard Cave

The colossal caverns of the Ozark Plateau tend to steal all the ink when it comes to what's written about caves in Missouri. There's plenty of hype heralding such beautiful show caves as Marvel, Bridal or Onondaga.

It probably will come as a surprise, then, to learn of the numerous caves found in Missouri's southeastern counties that hug the mighty Mississippi River. In fact, Perry County boasts the most caves of any county in the entire state with more than 650.

To the south of Perry County, the river county of Cape Girardeau can claim almost 50 caves. To the north of Perry County, the rolling hills of Ste. Genevieve County contain additional caverns. One of those Ste. Genevieve caves has been transformed into a wine cellar and an amazing location to share a bottle of vino. The cave is the focal point for Cave Vineyard.

Originally named Salt Peter Cave from an earlier era of French settlers, the cave today accommodates grape enthusiasts intent on settling in with a bottle of Chardonel or Traminette, Chambourcin or Cynthiana/Norton. On weekdays, a brook inside the cave babbles. On weekends, bands fill the Ste. Genevieve cave with Cajun, rock and country music entertainment.

Unfortunately, few caves in the state's southeast river counties offer the kind of open hospitality provided by Cave Vineyard. Most of the caves are closed to the general public. They are the province of caving experts, who make special arrangements with the cave owners for exploration parties.

Four of the five longest caves in Missouri are in Perry County, with Crevice Cave snaking below the green earth for a length of 28 miles. These caves are not for casual visitation. Explorers must have proper training along with the necessary equipment.

These netherworld tunnels require extra precautions, in part because they are subject to flash flooding. Heavy rains enter the caves through a maze of sinkholes, steep ravines, dry creek beds and intentionally excavated holes made by man.

Man-made holes and some natural sinkholes have been used for years as septic tanks, garbage dumps, cattle and hog waste disposals and worse. In wicked storms, these caves can overflow with a sickly mulligan stew of oil, chemicals, pesticides, fertilizers and many other pollutants.

Ethical cavers are among the folks battling to end this environmental abuse. They will tell you that these little-known caves can be as spectacular as any of the Ozark show caves when conditions are right.

Perhaps you'd like to join a grotto club or spelunking group to learn how to safely explore this vast cave network of Missouri's southeastern counties. If not, at least consider a trip to Cave Vineyard in Ste. Genevieve. There, you can lift a toast to all cavers who are working to stop the degradation and to preserve an underground heritage.

JUST SPECIAL PLACES

IV

MANY ENCHANTING NATURE SPOTS IN THE HEARTLAND DEFY CATEGORIZATION AS BLUFF, SPRING, STREAM OR CAVERN. Some sites may consist of a stubborn stand of old-growth trees; or a strange collection of massive granite rocks; or a humble swatch of wildflowers in a rehabbed prairie glade. In any case, they all might rightly count as natural wonders.

Perhaps the best way to classify these outdoor locations is to label them as "just special places." All of these sites offer their own unique opportunities for physical recreation, mental relaxation, holistic happiness and spiritual rejuvenation.

These are special places which may not have the broad vistas of a rocky cliff outcropping, or the wild energy of a mighty spring, or the dark secrets of a deep, mysterious cave. Yet, these nature sites are most assuredly special places. They have a natural magnetism that draws a wide array of human beings intent on finding some magical refuge.

Certainly, Elephant Rocks State Park counts as a nature site that refuses to conform to any ready classification. The park's incredible billion-year-old boulders were once quarried to furnish building blocks for St. Louis streets and the city's famous Eads Bridge. Fortunately, these once-endangered stone beasts are now a protected herd in a visitor-friendly environment.

Two nature locations, specially selected for inclusion in this volume, have everything to do with trees. The first site, Big Oak Tree State Park, provides a glimpse into the vast bottomland forest which covered the Missouri Bootheel in a not-so-distant past. This arbor island of big oaks is all that's left of a continuous midcontinent forest that was cut down and ruthlessly logged in the early 20th century.

The trees of Knob Noster in the western part of Missouri are pale tea compared to the tall timber survivors of Big Oak Tree State Park. Even so, a forest walk through the new growth trees of Knob Noster State Park, particularly during the blustery seasons of fall and spring, can be downright disturbing—and mystical.

At Knob Noster, during those bewitching seasons of windy change, crunchy leaves blow and chatter around exposed tree roots while the lanky tree limbs above are set in motion. They communicate a branch of sign language intelligible only to those who willingly give nature the time of day.

Another natural wonder site, where great trees have wise tales to tell, is the Allred Lake Natural Area. Among the trees that emerge from the muck of the Allred swamp are tupelo gum and bald cypress. A goodly number of the knobby-kneed cypress are said to date from pre-Columbian times—that's before 1492.

Situated in an isolated part of southeastern Missouri, Allred Lake Natural Area requires a bit of distant travel for most visitors. Some distant time travel via the imagination also may be required to truly appreciate this place. Allred's looks easily inspire primeval visions.

Natural curiosities such as Big Oak Tree State Park, Allred Lake Natural

Area, the Mississippi River's Tower Rock, the great split rock of Grand Gulf State Park and Elephant Rocks all require extensive use of the internal combustion engine as well as bipedal locomotion in order to effect a close-up visit. However, not all special places require demanding travel.

Many special places may be much closer to home, especially if you happen to be a resident of one of Missouri's two great metropolises, St. Louis or Kansas City. If St. Louisans want a taste of primordial past, Mastodon State Park is minutes away versus the hours it takes to get to Allred Lake near the Arkansas border. The bone bed at the St. Louis–area state park has coughed up the relics of mastodons and ground sloths from more than 25,000 years ago.

Residents of the St. Louis region can take pride in having rallied together to save significant spaces for transformation into special places. A classic example of this effort is found at Route 66 State Park. Once the dioxin-contaminated EPA environmental disaster site known as Times Beach, today this pleasant land along the Meramec River has been reclaimed as a nature haven.

Farther down the Meramec River are the beautiful outdoor sites of Powder Valley Nature Center and Emmenegger Nature Park in southwest suburban St. Louis. Both of these stretches of wildland were destined to become subdivision developments. Nearby residents, landowners and public agencies worked together to find alternatives to more development.

Powder Valley Nature Center now offers a host of outdoor educational activities and a popular meeting site for cavers, birders, butterfly watchers, conservationists and naturalists. Emmenegger Nature Park and Powder Valley also provide woodland hikes tailored for both the strong of leg and the faint of heart.

Kansas City folks, just like St. Louisans, have been organizing to rescue and nurture natural wonder spots within their own urban maze. Environmental groups such as the Kansas City Wildlands have identified remnants of forest, tall grass prairie, healthy bottomland, as well as glades and savannas that should be secured and protected for future generations.

Friends of the Lakeside Nature Center in Kansas City's Swope Park have put together nature walks through prairie vegetation, upland savannas and along rocky chert cliffs. Those walks have awakened interest in the city's vast underlying shelf of Bethany Falls Limestone and curiosity about the natural history of these layers of gray shale, which date back 300 million years or more.

Kansas Citians have gone to work to rescue their Blue River, which has long suffered the indignity of serving as the community dumpster. River rescuers have pinpointed many spots along the Blue that are ecologically valuable and also priceless as scenic respites for the tired eyes of the harried urban dweller.

There may not always be time for the urban dweller to make trips to inspirational outdoor sites, even when they are as close as a local conservation nature center or a forested neighborhood park. This doesn't have to be an unsolvable problem. If the spirit is willing, but circumstances involving time and transportation get in the way, then consider other options.

Consider creating a special natural haven right in your own backyard. Plenty of informational resources and expert help are available to create special spaces at home. Build it, and nature will surely come—perhaps in the form of hardy perennial plants and wildflowers; perhaps in the form of birds, bees and butterflies.

Shaw Nature Reserve in Gray Summit boasts numerous wildflower trails and 800 species of plants in the renowned Whitmore Wildflower Garden near the Bascom House. At Shaw, aspiring gardeners can learn about all the growing essentials for native perennials, vines, grasses, shrubs, flowering trees and many more living things. Shaw Nature Reserve is owned by the world-famous Missouri Botanical Garden. The Garden's experts conduct classes on native plants and how to cultivate a native plant garden.

Of course, if you're looking for some backyard nature that is both visual and aural, you may want to consult with the birders. A good place to find bird lovers is at the Little Creve Coeur Wetlands, which has become a favorite stop for migratory fowl using the Mississippi Flyway.

Little Creve Coeur Wetlands is a marsh restoration project with the support of the Sierra Club, Missouri Coalition for the Environment and those birders— the Audubon Society. Audubon Society members bring their cameras, tripods and telescopes to the wetlands to monitor the project's success in attracting birds.

The birders will know you're serious about their avocation if you join them with a set of binoculars at Little Creve Coeur Wetlands. Many of them have backyard bird sanctuaries at their own homes. The Audubon folks will be happy to offer up their secrets in building a backyard bird habitat—after some shared bird watching at the wetlands.

Another binocular-toting group willing to help turn a backyard into a nature refuge is the North American Butterfly Association (NABA). The butterfly gang will tell you that their favorite winged creatures are easy to attract, lots of fun to watch, and a colorful complement for any backyard garden. That garden, of course, must be specially designed for butterflies.

A real butterfly garden will look a bit ragged around the edges, since its main purpose is to serve as food for larval butterflies. The key to success is to cultivate native plants that butterflies love: butterfly bush, blue indigo, prairie blazing star, shining blue star, columbine and many varieties of milkweed.

For gardening information and for inspiration, the Missouri Botanical Garden oversees the Butterfly House in Chesterfield, west of St. Louis. A classic garden to enjoy and to emulate is the Elizabeth Danforth Butterfly Garden on the campus of Washington University in St. Louis. The St. Louis Zoo's impressive Insectarium is yet another resource for education on butterflies and butterfly gardening.

In St. Charles County, the Jim Ziebol Butterfly Garden at Busch Conservation Area demonstrates how to attract butterflies with nectar and host plant sources. The special field site is a joint project of NABA, the Missouri Department of Conservation and the Webster Groves Nature Society.

This writer stands in awe and admiration of those who find the energy to convert a backyard plot into habitat for wildflowers, birds or butterflies. These homegrown nature spots are not only aesthetically pleasing, but they also play a part in repairing a web of life torn asunder in the name of progress.

ALLRED LAKES CYPRESS SWAMP

JUNGIAN PSYCHOLOGISTS TALK ABOUT MAN'S COLLECTIVE UNCONSCIOUS, WHERE BITS OF MEMORY ARE STORED FROM EONS OF OUR EVOLUTIONARY DEVELOPMENT.

At some distant point on the way to becoming human, our early ancestors crawled out of the primordial swamp to become land creatures. If you want to get a glimpse at what that swamp might have looked like, you couldn't do better than to take a gander at the Allred Lake Natural Area in the bootheel area of southeast Missouri.

Allred Lake is as primordial as it gets in the state. Its primitive scenery may actually inspire a bit of deja vu from the old collective unconscious first described by Carl Jung.

If you feel a chill and are creeped out as dusk falls at Allred, it could be that Jungian thing. After all, crawling out of a place like this must have been extremely traumatic—some real bad memories probably had their genesis back at that original evolutionary swamp.

So, what makes Allred so creepy?

Well, first of all, it is a swamp. It's dark and dank. The place hums with mosquitoes in the depths of summer, when its hellish heat and humidity rival any Louisiana Bayou.

Then there are the strange beasts of the swamp, such as the slithery siren intermedia. Classified as the most archaic line of salamander still alive on the planet, sirens are eel-like creatures that scientists say wriggled below the primordial ooze more than a quarter-billion years ago.

Joining the siren intermedia at Allred are two equally antique specimens hailing from the fish world—the gars and bowfins. These two ugly, finned, nocturnal feeders are virtually unchanged from the time when great dinosaurs roamed the earth.

Bowfins are known for sharp rows of teeth used to tear apart more desirable fish. Gars also have elongated jaws full of sharp teeth that cause mayhem for any critters which have adapted to these intolerable marine conditions.

What really gives Allred its totally antedilluvin character are the giant bald cypress trees, some which date back to pre-Columbian times. Bald cypress are anchored by swollen trunks with "knees" set right above the swampy surface.

This writer's first encounter with bald cypress was years ago in a brackish swamp in South Carolina. Like many Missourians, I then had no idea that such a primitive swamp could be found in our own backyard.

Looking out on Allred, it's hard to believe that this weird, water-logged acreage was once typical of millions of acres of southeast Missouri. Hunters, farmers and lumberjacks came along to drain the swamps and to forever alter the area's entire ecosystem.

Seeing Allred, it's easy to understand why some folks prefer the Genesis story to evolution. It's also easy to see why early settlers had no qualms about draining our swamp lands, but in doing so, they destroyed a natural legacy.

BIG OAK TREE STATE PARK

MINNESOTA'S MYTHICAL LUMBERJACK, PAUL BUNYAN, MUST HAVE HAD A SIBLING IN SOUTHEAST MISSOURI. Let's call him Billy "Bootheel" Bunyan, because the state's bootheel area is where his work was carried out with an apparent fervor that defies the imagination.

A dense forest of tall, old-growth hardwoods once blanketed this area, renowned as a buggy, soggy, swamp-infested lowland. Logging companies began tearing away at this thick tree blanket early in the 1880s, and by the Great Depression, literally hundreds of thousands of forested acres were leveled.

Most of this "swampeast" region today is a vast, flattened patchwork of cotton fields and farm crops. As you drive through Mississippi County, however, an apparition appears south of the small town of East Prairie. It's an island of trees, an oasis of tallish timber standing in a sea of soybeans.

The 1,029-acre tract, known as Big Oak Tree State Park, preserves a landscape out of time that looks eerily primordial in contrast to the nearby countryside. An 80-acre tract of original virgin forest sits within the boundaries of the state park.

A history of the tree park's creation is at once inspiring, and sobering, for it's a story of how the last vestige of the great hardwood forest barely escaped the chainsaw. Mississippi County residents became fired up to save their remaining natural heritage in the 1930s, after they learned of the area's rare champion trees—trees of superior girth, height and crown. Among those trees was a 143-feet tall oak—its trunk more than 20-feet wide—with more than three centuries of growing history under its bark.

The successful campaign to save the last piece of giant forest enlisted school children who collected pennies; businesses which provided dollars; and small-town and big-city newspapers which supported the cause with ink.

Alas, while the "forest" was saved, the tree of trees was eventually lost. It succumbed to great bolts of lightning, rather than meeting its demise at the hands of old Billy "Bootheel" Bunyan. After the big bur oak's death, it was sawed down in 1954. A cross section of the monster tree still remains displayed in a glass case today.

When you visit the tree park, you'll find a new, half-mile long boardwalk through the park forest. On your hike, you'll be able to observe both state and national champion trees.

If hiking with children, you can entertain them with tall tales of Paul and Billy Bunyan. You can ask them to guess how many whacks of their axe were needed to fell a champion.

If hiking with adults, you can pose that age-old question: If a tree falls in the forest with no one to hear it, then does it make a sound? Also consider this: If an entire forest is demolished, and there is not even a small park of trees left in its remembrance, did the forest ever exist?

BLUE RIVER PARKWAY

WHAT IS A NATURE EXPERIENCE? Is it the feel of a cool, blue stream flowing over tired, bare feet? Is it a surprise for the eyes of an endless horizon atop a bluff just scaled? Is it the gurgling sounds of a bubbly spring finding ears accustomed to an urban staccato?

Actually, nature's aesthetic experiences include these and much, much more. And not all great inspirational encounters with nature are passive. Some involve just getting plain "down and dirty" in the great outdoors.

Just ask the folks with Blue River Rescue in Kansas City. They wade through the waters of the Blue every year to pull out cans, bottles, tires, stoves, refrigerators, dumpsters and abandoned autos. Blue River Rescue volunteers number 900, and they have retrieved as much as 220 tons of trash from their beleaguered urban stream.

Blue River is not much to look at when driving over the I-70 bridge that takes you into Kansas City. It might be more aptly tagged as "Dank River" at that point—a mere mud canal—delivering storm water, urban effluent and real nasty runoff to the Missouri River to its north.

However, south of the interstate, Blue River is being reclaimed. Nature folks are working to restore it to an Ozark stream quality. Restoration is an uphill battle, because every year the river is subject to degradation and abuse. Blue River Rescue has made progress by blocking access roads that once allowed dumpers to do their dirty deeds under cover of darkness.

Rescue folks aren't the only ones true to the river Blue. Volunteers with Kansas City Wildlands work to weed out honeysuckle, garlic mustard and other invasive plants that threaten forest, river habitat and the integrity of the banks of the river Blue.

Bush honeysuckle destroys the undergrowth on the river that often prevents silt and soil from filling its waters. Spring canoeists experience water riffles on the rocks in some sections of the Blue, thanks to volunteers on Ecological Restoration Days.

Blue River nature lovers are transforming its upstream areas into safer habitat for fish species, ranging from the common sunfish to orangethroat darters, red shiners and stonerollers. Above the water's surface, owls, woodpeckers and cuckoos also are enjoying the habitat improvements wrought by the volunteer nature workers.

Of course, the enjoyment is not all one way. Humans find benefit in both the teamwork of outdoor restoration and in the aesthetic results of their labors. Nature nurturers profess feelings of intense gratification when they look over a stretch of river or nearby forest area in recovery.

"After a day of mud and sweat, you get satisfaction to see nature on the mend," said a Wildlands volunteer. "You feel a sense of ownership of the river— you don't want anybody jacking with it. And the disrespect shown for nature becomes an ethical issue."

Ibby's Butterfly Garden

Ibby's Garden on the campus of Washington University, more formally known as the Elizabeth Danforth Butterfly Garden, provides a perfect example of how nature can be lured to your own backyard. You don't always have to go out, or trek about, to spend time in the company of nature.

Ibby's Garden bloomed for three reasons: to honor the matriarch of the university; to provide the community with a refuge from everyday stress and pressures; and to make available a source of food for dwindling numbers of pollinators—specifically butterflies—in an urban environment.

Butterfly gardens, butterfly houses and butterfly conservation areas have become more and more popular in the decade since the garden for Elizabeth Danforth was first dedicated in 1996. Some St. Louis–area butterfly projects are larger than Ibby's Garden, while others thrive in corners of backyards abutting modest bungalows.

The important thing is that the butterflies are oblivious to all fanfare and ostentation. They're simply looking for a few good flowers—some drought-tolerant, nectaring plants—and the right habitat to launch their fitful and flighty short careers.

Numerous plants adorn the typical garden, plantings to attract both wily caterpillars and the prized, sought-after, delicate-winged creatures. A garden should contain woody plants and perennials and annuals, such as coneflowers, milkweed, periwinkle, snapdragons, marigolds and more.

Butterflies are easy to attract; they fill the air with fun colors while they seek out their own preferred colors. They are able to identify pinks, yellows, whites and purplish hues of their favorite flowers.

Butterflies must raise their body temperatures in order to fly. After a cool morning, they often will alight on flowers, shrubs and flat surfaces to absorb heat from the sun. Once their bodies reach 86 degrees Fahrenheit or more, they are ready to take flight.

If you think butterflies can be both mysterious and beautiful, you are not alone. Throughout the ages, they have been the focus of myths, legends, poems, fairytales, superstitions and artforms for many diverse cultures. Symbols of death and rebirth, butterflies have appeared in the poetry of Blake, in paintings by Picasso and in ritual dances of Native Americans.

An abundance of butterflies in a community points to the well-being of its ecosystem. So, the butterfly is now a modern symbol for our fragile ecology as well as for scientific complexity.

The late scientist Carl Sagan once used butterflies in reference to the enormous amounts of time required by evolution. He said our resistance to Darwin stems from our difficulty to imagine the eons: "What does 70 million years mean to beings who live only one-millionth as long? We are like butterflies who flutter for a day and think it is forever."

Trailblazing Chubb Trail

My first experience with mountain biking was at Keystone in Colorado at a nephew's wedding. I can still recall the frazzled look on the fellow's face at the bike rental store when I asked whether it was really necessary to wear a helmet while mountain biking.

After a quick ride up a gondola ski lift to Keystone's summit, I spent hours on the bike brakes trying to negotiate zig-zag pathways back down to the bottom. Admittedly, there were several enjoyable interludes on this adventure in the company of deer and moose.

Before reaching Keystone's base, one of my nephews hit a boulder and went over the handlebars. His head hit another rock upon his landing, cracking his helmet but, fortunately, not his skull. He was pretty beat up when he stood up for his brother a few hours later in the wedding.

After my Keystone mountain biking adventure, I was reasonably sure I would not encounter the sport again anytime soon. After all, mountains of the Colorado variety are hard to come by for folks living among the tamer hills and valleys of Missouri.

Then, one summer morning, I was hiking Chubb Trail about 15 miles southwest of St. Louis. This trail on the south side of the Meramec River has some tough, steep terrain. Porous rocks resembling giant stone sponges are partially buried along the trail.

While stooping to examine one of these large sponge meteors embedded in my pathway, I was startled to hear a voice from some place warning me: "Behind you, sir, mountain biker."

While I stepped aside, the biker was compelled to "portage" his mean mountain machine over the spongy rock section of the trail. This gave me an opportunity to converse with him about St. Louis–area mountain biking.

Chubb Trail and its companion paths in West Tyson Park are among the most popular for mountain bikers. They are favored because they hook up with trails in adjacent Castlewood Park to the north and Lone Elk Park to the east. This makes for miles of scenic bike travel in the forests and glades of the Meramec River Valley.

Backcountry biking provides a way to cover more territory and to experience more of nature in a shorter time than hiking allows. Along Chubb and its adjacent trails, this can mean "eye treats" such as forest and river valley landscapes as well as animals, ranging from fox, deer and turkey to geese, duck, eagle and heron.

Some hikers are less than pleased to be sharing their sacred places with mountain bikers. This need not be. Folks who pound the ground should be natural allies with those who pedal mountain metal. Both share a common code of the trail that, when followed, can be mutually beneficial.

Among the points of etiquette: be polite, make way for others; leave no trace behind; avoid spooking animals; take safety precautions—wear a helmet if you visit nature on wheels.

CLAIRE GEMPP DAVIDSON PARK

TUCKED AWAY IN A BUSTLING, AFFLUENT ST. LOUIS SUBURB IS A 13-ACRE OASIS OF FLORA AND FAUNA, FOREST AND PRAIRIE. An added surprise, deep within the small forest perimeter, is a wetlands pond full of water lilies, frogs and turtles.

Ordinarily, a fine swatch of land like this would be snatched up by a developer for some rezoning, platting and plotting. It would then be raked over, rendered flat, and delivered over for the latest creations of the McMansion builders of greater suburbia.

How did this nature refuge, located in the midst of sprawling malls and miscellaneous thoroughfares, come to exist? How was it spared the bulldozer, the concrete pourer, the itinerant home construction crew's outhouse?

Divine intervention might be one explanation but, in fact, the Claire Gempp Memorial Conservation Area is the result of a grande dame's donation. Once part of a large dairy farm, the land was ceded to the Missouri Department of Conservation by Marjorie Elizabeth Gempp in her will—in the name of her younger sister.

Today, this most unique, ex-urban, environmental enterprise is managed in a one-of-a-kind relationship by the state conservation department, the suburb of Sunset Hills and the local Lindbergh School District. All three entities benefit from this arrangement.

However, the greatest beneficiaries may be the area students who come to Claire Gempp to learn about prairie plants and flowers; to tally the species of wildlife frequenting the area; to witness the change in seasons that has inspired both prose and poetry.

Claire Gempp's thriving patch of nature can be an outdoor resource for students of any age. One of its many pleasures is to sit on the south edge of its pond on a breezy day. There, you can look up into the trees and watch a wind symphony. Broad leafs provide the bass, while the rippling slender-leafed species provide a shrill treble.

When the winds die down, and the conductor takes his leave, you can take a walk. Along the trails, educational panel signs offer insights on nature. "Hey! You Don't Belong Here," screams one panel. Humans are not the target of this admonition but, instead, the dread bush honeysuckle.

- It's very aggressive and quickly crowds out other flowers and plants.
- It's roots contain a toxin that can slow or stop growth of other plants.
- It dramatically changes the character and understory of the forest.

Bush honeysuckle was introduced in America as a vigorous ornamental that could provide a quick, easy growth of hedge. Left unchecked, though, it began to spread, and its success now seems to threaten every tree and wild flower.

One of the students' major goals at Claire Gempp now is to remove honeysuckle from the park, to save some habitat for native trees and flowers. It's a goal consistent with the original mission of Claire Gempp—to save a bit of space from encroaching growth.

CREVE COEUR WETLANDS

CIVILIZED MAN PAYS DUTIFUL RESPECT AND HOMAGE TO THE ACRONYMS THAT HE HAS CREATED. MANY OF THESE ACRONYMS STAND FOR HUGE GOVERNMENT BUREAUCRACIES, RANGING FROM THE FBI TO THE DOE TO FEMA.

However, some new acronyms that have popped up are actually prized by less-than-civilized folks—the back-to-nature types. One of these new-fangled alphabet combinations for nature lovers is IBA, which stands for Important Bird Area.

Unfortunately, bird areas have become more critical, as they have dwindled in number. Two centuries of civilization in North America have led to a marked decline in the wetlands acreage once available to birds.

The length of the Mississippi River is one of the four major "flyways" for migrating birds in North America. Swamplands, oxbows and tributaries along the river once provided many flyway "rest stops" for birds for thousands of years.

Farmers drained this habitat to make way for agriculture. Municipal authorities drained these lowland areas for wharfs and industrial parks. Developers drained these wetlands areas for malls and subdivisions.

In Missouri, almost 95 percent of the original wetlands in the state has been lost. Such staggering losses have prompted some folks to work for wetlands restoration, in part, to establish IBAs.

An important bird area also can be an important people area. This fact becomes obvious when you visit the IBA-designated site of Little Creve Coeur Wetlands, located in west St. Louis County.

You know the people at this site are doing important things when you see them assembled with their tripods, telescopes and binoculars. These folks are likely to be with the Audubon Society, and they're happy to let you have a zoom-lens peak at the birds.

"There's a red-winged blackbird nest in the cattails," you'll hear one of the birders say, while peering through the scope on its tripod. "I start by just looking for an unusual lump, and often it turns out to be a nest when you use the focus."

There is excitement among the birders when they spot bitterns, marsh wrens, least terns and other species that are threatened or endangered. You may find the excitement to be contagious if you choose to hike the trail to this birder haven between Creve Coeur Lake and the Missouri River.

The St. Louis County Parks Department has been working to restore and expand the Creve Coeur marsh areas, with plenty of input from groups which include the Sierra Club, Audubon Society and the Coalition for the Environment.

Birders say Little Creve Coeur Wetlands is picking up as a major "stop" on the Mississippi route for migrating bird species. Humans may find the refurbished wetlands area to be a pretty good rest stop as well.

Devil's Toll Gate

Few natural phenomena are as intimidating as a Missouri electrical storm. Jagged bolts of lightning join reverberating booms of thunder to deliver harsh ultimatums to puny earth-bound souls.

Missourian Mark Twain wrote that when he was a boy, he would curl up in his bed in terror when fierce thunderstorms came upon Hannibal in the middle of the night. Amidst the nocturnal melee, he would admit all his transgressions and beg the Almighty's forgiveness. He hoped his confession would somehow get the storm to pass.

It should not be surprising that lightning and thunder figure heavily in the region's folklore, long before Twain and the arrival of his ancestors from Europe. Taum Sauk Mountain near Ironton is a locale of Native American legends—lightning and thunder play leads in these stories.

The fable of the maiden of the Valley of Flowers is such a tale. The maiden lived with a nomadic tribe that roamed the valley. She was curious about what might live at the top of Taum Sauk, though the tribal elders forbade her to consider the climb.

One hot summer day, curiosity got the best of her. She had heard of a cooling falls at the mountain top, and near dusk she decided to try to find it. Storm clouds closed in as she neared the top. Approaching thunder brought on panic. As she frantically looked for a path down the mountain, she realized that a revolting, sloth-like figure was following her and drawing closer.

She began to run, only to come up against a tall, flat granite wall. The maiden knew she was trapped, and she cried out in fear and desperation. Just then, a blinding bolt of lightning crashed against the granite.

Just as the God of Moses divided the sea, the lightning split the rock in two, and the maiden escaped through a chasm. Today, it is possible to trek through the same narrow, eight-foot defile that saved the maiden.

When passing through the toll gate, remember that the name Devil's Toll Gate is not derived from the maiden legend. It actually draws its name from its use as an old trail to the territory of the Southwest. Cargo on wagons taking this route would often have to be unloaded, re-stacked and balanced to make it through the narrow passage. Hence, the devil collected his toll.

It is said the Cherokee had to sadly pay the devil his due in 1838–39 on a forced migration to harsher lands in the West. The route of the forced march of the Cherokees is today known as the Trail of Tears. Many Cherokee elderly, women and children died in that horrific resettlement.

The wonder of Mina Sauk includes not only its ancient earthly mountain, but also cloud mountains assembling to unleash fury. If, as a visitor, you encounter this clashing of high land and lowered sky, think beyond the Valley of Flowers maiden's rescue. The skies may be opening up in indignation because of the Cherokees' sad fate. Appreciating nature's righteous anger may offer a path to deliverance from past evil—a route to absolution.

Elephant Rocks

Europeans came to America to conquer a new land, to harvest fields, to cut timber, to mine its minerals. They came to the Ozarks and mined lead, tungsten and more mundane materials such as granite and limestone.

The aftermath of their exploits has not always been pretty—abandoned mine shafts, crumbling kilns, polluted quarry pools and slag heaps. Just as there are ghost towns from the Gold Rush days out West, the Ozark region has its share of decaying and dead outposts which once prospered.

Graniteville, a few miles south of Potosi on Missouri Highway 21, was a thriving town in the late 1800s. Built and owned by a quarry company, the mining town had a hotel, post office, school, general store and rail depot. Today, it is a shell of its former self.

The quarry workers, who mined the granite for bridges, columns, piers, cobblestones and gravestones, are long gone. Just outside one of the larger vacated quarries, south of aging Graniteville, can be found the oddest geological formations known collectively as Elephant Rocks.

How did these ancient rocks escape the pick axe, the chisel and hammer of the industry's quarry masters? Did their vast size, herd-like assembly and their mysterious aura ward off those who might have been tempted to round them up, break their spirit and ship them off to civilization?

Now protected by the Missouri Department of Natural Resources, the giant boulders are recognized for their outstanding geologic value. Their origins are traced to volcanoes erupting here 1.5 billion years ago.

The patriarch of the Elephant Rocks herd stands 27 feet tall, 35 feet long and 17 feet wide. Weighing 680 tons, this mammoth has experienced the same erosion and weathering that has rounded and smoothed the others in the pinkish pachyderm pack.

Fortunately, it's not essential to know all of their pre-Cambrian history to appreciate the timeless quality of these peculiar elephants. Neither is it necessary to know the official census of the herd, nor the dimensions of all the various members.

When you come to Elephant Rocks, leave your Western mind, with its obsession for the flotsam and jetsam of detail, far behind. Forget about those who came a century earlier, with minds calculating the means to fracture, lift up and remove these marvels of a quiet earth to the cities.

Instead, come to Elephant Rocks and prepare to embrace their ancient mystery as well as their here-and-now physical existence. An extraordinary way to enjoy the rocks is through the tactile senses—try the fingertips.

On a sunny day, climb upon a rock that fits the contour of your body, so you make contact with as much warm rock as physically possible. Rest with rock. Become one with it. Convey your appreciation through your happy fingertips.

Emmenegger's Urban Holler

A HOLLOW IS A SMALL, DEEP VALLEY THAT IS SQUEEZED BETWEEN TWO MOUNTAINS. Some dictionaries contend such geographic phenomena are commonly found in the Appalachians, but those places are "hollers," not hollows.

Genuine hollows can occasionally be found in the Midwest, especially in the Ozarks, but generally not in populated areas. One place to experience an urban, microcosmic hollow is at the Emmenegger Nature Park near the northwest corner of Interstates 44 and 270 in St. Louis County.

Most folks visiting this park tend to follow a pathway along the river to enjoy the flowing Meramec. It's a great place to skip rocks on the water. Visitors also seem to favor climbing a trail to the Meramec bluffs, where they can see a blue sky meet with a hilly, green horizon on a summer day.

However, sandwiched between the river bluffs on the west and a steep hillside that abuts I-270 on the east side of the park is an urban hollow of sorts. Like a miniature Appalachian "holler," its geography shields it from sunlight both morning and evening. In the summer, its impressive tree canopy lets even less light through.

Perhaps it's no surprise that an unassuming creek, a small tributary of the Meramec, meanders through the hollow. Most of the time, it flows as a trickle. With melting snow, spring rains or summer downpours, it can become something more impressive.

So why lollygag in this dark, dank, humid, urban microcosm of a hollow? Why travel down this mulched trail which sometimes simply transforms into muddy bottomland? Why? Because this unlikely locale can occasionally provide the quintessential experience of nature.

If you want to enjoy the Emmenegger hollow at its best, try to time your visit with the arrival of a weather front. Thanks to the information provided by today's Weather Channel, this kind of meteorological encounter is no longer serendipitous—it can be planned.

Enter the park hollow about one-half hour before a storm front is about to arrive. Preferably, this will be on a hot, humid, late summer afternoon or early evening, when Midwest storms are quite famous for firing up.

Initially, you will feel rivulets of sweat pouring down your neck, and your eyes will smart from a salty concoction drooling from your brows. All will be still. Then, suddenly, many flat leaves in the tree canopy will begin to stir. A rushing sound, like a waterfall, will fill the air and your ears.

Huge branches will begin to twist and scream in the wind. Your sweat will evaporate to a dry salt in the cooling breeze. You may even get chills as darkness overtakes and consumes this small forest outpost. The storm has arrived.

This experience is at once awesome and invigorating, frightening and refreshing. Congratulate yourself. You are a witness to one of nature's best shows on the strange stage of an urban hollow.

GRAND GULF

FOR MY GAS-GUZZLING MONEY, GRAND GULF IS ONE OF THE MOST BIZARRE—AND BEAUTIFUL—GEOLOGIC WONDERS IN ALL OF MISSOURI. The trip is worth a tank or two of petrol, as well as the backroads travel time it may take to get there.

Located near the Missouri and Arkansas border, just west of a town called Thayer, Grand Gulf is the gemstone of a 322-acre state park. What exactly is this gemstone? It's a sinkhole, a collapsed cavern, a deep gorge, a natural bridge, a gaping wound or "gulf" in the Ozark earth.

The gulf itself stretches for almost one mile. Its walls of 130 feet or more create a yawning abyss, a chasm that has inspired local folks to call this Missouri's "Little Grand Canyon." Several boardwalks and overlooks have been built for edge-cliff views and for a partial descent into the canyon.

For a view from below, consider the Canyon Trail, which provides safe passage along the canyon floor. For a view from on high, consider walking the 200-foot span of Grand Gulf's natural bridge, perhaps the largest such feature in Missouri.

Geologists date the origins of Grand Gulf to more than 450 million years ago when sediments from receding seas consolidated into dolomite. The hard dolomite rock was fractured and hollowed by springs, streams and weather-related water flows.

At some point, the massive roof of the resulting cave system collapsed in a slew of boulders and debris. The roof collapse is so recent in geologic terms—perhaps 10,000 years ago—that geologists say the detrital slopes of the chasm are not yet stabilized.

It must have taken an apocalyptic upheaval to make the roof cave in and the rock walls crash at Grand Gulf. Perhaps it was some cosmic Samson, visiting from another galaxy, who pushed the walls apart to cause the calamity. A more plausible explanation might involve a colossal eruption of the New Madrid fault with an earthquake of prehistoric proportions.

Of course, it's not necessary to go back thousands of years to trace unprecedented disaster at the Grand Gulf. During the 1890s, a stretch of remaining cave at Grand Gulf was explored by the curious by boat. Those deep explorations ceased in 1921 after a terrible tornado and flood.

The great storm's torrents of water washed downed trees and loose rock into the great gulf, damming the cave entrance. The cave became impassable. Today, heavy rains can turn the gulf into a lake, which drains slowly through the blocked portion of cavern.

If you visit Grand Gulf and ponder a while on its prominent overlook deck, imagine the great quakes and the storm fronts this place has seen. Which would you rather witness firsthand?

With sincere apologies to Robert Frost: "Some say the world will end in quake; some say in squall. It must have taken a mighty something, to cause the roof to fall"—at Grand Gulf.

Blue River Glades Natural Area

Under a sunny sky in late fall or early spring, there is no greater pleasure than to sprawl out on a smooth boulder sporting a southwest exposure. Rock warmth readily trasmits to a body at rest and provides a needed antidote to chilly, seasonal breezes.

On a visit to Kansas City, I found some good rock warmth in the Blue River Glades Natural Area, south of Swope Park on the city's west side. The nature area is not well-marked, but the friendly folks at Swope Park's Lakeside Nature Center tipped me off to the nature site and how to find it.

An empty parking area on the side of Blue River Road indicated I had this place all to myself. It was a nice Saturday in early November, and this quiet seclusion was welcome, but also a source of concern.

The trails seemed overgrown, steep and dark, and far less-traveled than expected—and this gave me further pause. However, any anxiety melted away when the trail opened up to one large glade, and then another. These glades were covered with sunlight in contrast to the heavily shaded trails full of thick weeds and tall oaks.

It's easy to lose track of a trail in a glade. Glades are like open-air islands in the forest. They have thin layers of rocky soil, so they are usually host to wild grasses, brushy plants and hearty wildflowers. Trees do not do well here. Few survive to maturity.

Areas of growth in a glade are sometimes interrupted by exposed bedrock, cliffs and outcroppings. In the Swope Park area of Kansas City, the bedrock is called Bethany Falls limestone. It dates back 300 million years to the Pennsylvanian Period, when much of Missouri was under a shallow sea.

A number of glades, especially farther south in Missouri, are home to small scorpions, tarantulas and wily lizards. Such glade-loving creatures add to the southwestern feel of these open-air islands in a Midwest woods.

No scorpions, snakes or fleet-footed reptiles visited me while I stetched out for a late fall snooze at the River Glades Natural Area. However, it's easy to imagine that these denizens of desert-like climes would likely take up apartments here in August, when Kansas City thermometers surge far past the 90-degree threshold.

If you choose to visit Blue River Glades Natural Area, my suggestions lean to a fall or spring excursion. Rocky glades are for frying eggs in summer—best to come here when things simmer down a bit. Locals say the area bursts with blazing stars in September, plants whose nectar lures the migrating monarch butterflies.

So make your reservations for a reclining spell on a Bethany Rock, amidst the flutter of butterflies. Do it closer to fall. Find a piece of rock furniture that fits the contour of your figure. But go easy on this furniture. Show a little respect. After all, it's 300 million years old.

KNOB NOSTER TREES

TREES AND "PROGRESS" CAN SELDOM CO-EXIST. Trees are no match for bulldozers. Urban dwellers know well the sight of uprooted trees shoved to some plot's corner to make way for development. Such scenes of carnage can still send a shock to the system.

This writer was a passenger one day in the car of baseball great Stan Musial. On the way to a restaurant meeting, a tangled mass of bulldozed trees caught Musial's eye. He stopped his car, stepped out into the street, and surveyed the natural destruction wrought for a subdivision development.

I was impressed that my childhood hero could be touched so obviously by this natural destruction. I often think about Stan the Man's reaction when I pause to appreciate a stand of trees. "What a loss," I heard Stan lament.

One place in Missouri where the trees are not losing is Knob Noster State Park, roughly halfway between Warrensburg and Sedalia. The 3,567-acre park is located in a transition zone where the prairies meet the forests. This type of landscape is sometimes referred to as a savanna.

Knob Noster supports a number of walking trails, with northern jaunts that follow a meandering creek. My favorite trails are those reaching out into the Clearfork Savanna area. The terrain is populated with different species of oak, hickory, pawpaw, redbud, hackberry and more.

At Knob Noster, trees rule. You get a sense that you're on their turf, most notably if you hike alone—when few live souls are in the park. Interesting times to visit Knob Noster are in late fall or early spring, when humans are scarce and the trees dominate.

Leafless and barren, the trees still manage to whip in the wind because of their many small branches. Most are third growth timber that replaced the original wood growth in the savanna areas. As the limbs coil and recoil in the wind, they seem to reach out, as if to grab a solitary hiker.

Because the trees are spaced apart, they can be studied individually. Some look like old men with long noses. Large knots make for eyes. A bent treetop sprawl makes for a disheveled, hairy head. Of course, there are also those menacing limbs always reaching out to seize you.

The park can be a little creepy at these times, especially if the sky is growing heavy with dark clouds, particularly when the horizon melts into an awesome swarm of trees and more trees. These are not the grumpy trees that threw apples at Dorothy on the way to Oz. These trees are seriously angry—they mean business.

It's fun to let your imagination run away with you at Knob Noster. Native American mythology holds that two hills, or "knobs," were raised as monuments to slain warriors in this area where prairie meets forest. Perhaps their spirits still swirl with the gales that goad trees to lash out in anger.

Yes, at Knob Noster, trees rule. Go to their kingdom, if you dare.

MASTODON STATE PARK

AS A NATURAL AREA, MASTODON STATE PARK LEAVES A LOT TO BE DESIRED. Nearby Interstate 55 provides a constant roar of background noise. Vistas from the highest points in the park reveal boxy subdivision developments, strip malls, warehouses and fast food joints.

On a visit before the nation's birthday, you can add red, white and blue tents as part of the scenery. Cars on grass lots deliver up scads of shoppers ready to load up on snakes, sparklers and firecrackers sold under the tents.

While this 425-acre park property's immediate surroundings detract from its status as a natural refuge, it still qualifies as a special place that can inspire reflection, contemplation and meditation. That's because there is so much archeological and anthropological history at Mastodon State Park.

The entrance signage to the site, which features a welcoming, tusked mastodon, lets you know right away that this is no ordinary state nature park. A fiberglass skeleton of a giant, 20-foot-long, elephant-like mastodon in the park's museum center provides visitors with an idea of the animal life that once thrived in this region.

Bones of mastodons, ground sloths and peccaries, which roamed the area 25,000 years ago, were discovered in the nearby Kimmswick Bone Bed. The bone bed can be found behind the museum center. The bed site was once famous for the most impressive relics of the Pleistocene Ice Age era.

In 1979, the bone bed entered the annals of archeological history when a stone spear point, made by hunters of the Clovis culture, was found near mastodon bones. The discovery gave the first clear evidence that humans lived among these giant, prehistoric beasts thousands of years ago.

The museum center has a Clovis culture exhibit, archeological displays and a fine slide show. However, if these sorts of amenities are not exactly your idea of a nature park visit, then slip out the center's backdoor where you'll find the half-mile trail to the bone bed or pit area.

Tourists first started coming to the Kimmswick Bone Bed as far back as the 1904 World's Fair. Many of the bed fossils were sold, lost or destroyed. Missouri's Department of Natural Resources now has the bone bed area safely buried and in wait of site excavation at some future time.

The trail to the bone beds passes through wildflowers, an old quarry and down a limestone bluff to the bed area. Also available here is the Spring Branch Trail, which traverses a picnic area and along a small, trickling creek that flows from Bollefer Spring.

One way to contemplate the bone bed site is from a quarry rock perch—comparing present and past. Do you think the roar of trucks on I-55 would compare to a noisy mastodon facing a Clovis hunter? Do you think July 4th fireworks can compare to the crack of timber snapping under the weight of a full-grown mastodon in transit?

PICKLE SPRINGS

BE PREPARED TO ENCOUNTER HOODOO WHEN YOU EXPLORE THE FASCINATING FORESTED GORGE KNOWN AS THE PICKLE SPRINGS NATURAL AREA. Hoodoo is not exactly voodoo, but a little spellcasting can occur at Pickle Springs.

A hilly, 180-acre site west of Ste. Genevieve, the parking lot entrance to Pickle Springs is small, unimpressive, non-descript. You may wonder what the big deal is about this place, but all skepticism will evaporate as soon as you begin the hike on the two-mile "Trail Through Time."

Geological oddities crop up early and throughout the trail experience. These wonders can be traced to 500 million years ago, when sand deposits were cemented together by the work of weather and the elements. Curious sandstone formations were the result.

Along the trail, you will witness geologic features with names such as "The Slot," "Keyhole," "Owl's Den Bluff," the oh-so mysterious "Spirit Canyon" and the huge outcropping called "Dome Rock Overlook," which affords beautiful vistas to the south.

Also along the trail are hoodoos, strange rock pillars and sandstone mounds. Dome Rock Overlook, a high bluff between the moist, cool comfort of Spirit Canyon and the craggy chaos of Rockpile Canyon, is described by locals as one giant hoodoo.

Hoodoos are more commonly associated with the Badlands region of South Dakota, the Colorado Plateau and Bryce Canyon in Utah. The closest a mid-westerner can get to these unusual spires and totem-pole shaped rocks may well be the Pickle Springs Natural Area.

Hoodoos in western Utah can often exceed a ten-story building in height. Some geological purists contend that only the tallest creations should be called hoodoos; smaller towers should be called "hoodoo rocks." Hoodoos at Pickle Springs are on a more human scale and, yet, still can inspire awe.

A notable hoodoo in-the-making at Pickle Springs is the "Double Arches" formation. Its odd-shaped arches hold up a sandstone shelf. When that shelf inevitably collapses from erosion, two wonderful hoodoos will hopefully be left behind for Pickle's backpackers.

While hoodoo should not be confused with voodoo, Canadian wordsmith Bill Casselman contends that Native Americans picked up the "hoodoo" word from northwest fur trappers. Tribal peoples liked the term and used it to refer to terrible creatures and dark, evil forces.

According to tribal mythology, evil giants were turned into petrified hoodoos by the Great Spirit, because of their nasty deeds. Careless humans can awake the stone giants by being too loud and obnoxious.

A distraught hoodoo, rustled from centuries of slumber, is likely to retaliate against humans by throwing boulders their way. This mythology should not be taken lightly when hiking among all Pickle Springs' hoodoos. Enjoy them—do not disturb them!

Powder Valley Nature Center

Have we Americans lost the true meaning of Halloween? Halloween is supposed to be a time for tykes dressed in capes and masks. It's supposed to be a time for kids to learn to deal with all things that go bump in the night. It is, above all, a nature holiday, marking a time when outdoor life pulls up the blankets and readies for a long winter's sleep.

Instead, Halloween has morphed into an adult holiday. Hundreds of millions of dollars are spent on food and spirits—not the scary kind—for adult parties. Adults dress up and their parades celebrate a night of weirdness from the island of Key West to the bay of San Francisco.

One place where the meaning of Halloween was not forgotten, when my youngsters were growing up, is Powder Valley Nature Center. Known as an "urban oasis" for nature, the 112-acres of craggy, wooded land is located near the constant, whirring traffic of I-44 and I-270 in Missouri.

Managed by the Conservation Department, center volunteers knew how to do All Hallow's Eve right for kiddies. Folks at Powder Valley put together a "walk in the dark," complete with ghostly decorations, ghoulish lighting and ghastly creatures.

The conservation area has three major walking trails, a neat outdoor amphitheater and a topnotch indoor nature center. A trail decorated for Halloween already had the great asset of passing by scary ravines and slippery, rocky ridges.

The Halloween trail also took advantage of trail bridges, perfect places for demonic creatures to hang out. My kids were sent into shivers when an old troll came out from under one bridge, swinging a small lantern.

A troll, in case you don't know, is a shaggy sort of ogre with a long nose and a moss-like growth on his head. Your average troll can be pretty scary-looking and sometimes has the tail of a cow and the manners of a goat.

However, trolls at Powder Valley were a well-mannered bunch. When my kids met their first troll, he was very polite and was pleased to explain his Scandinavian origins. He noted that Halloween is a troll holiday. Trolls shun the sun. Sunlight will turn trolls into stone or make them explode.

Speaking of explosions, Powder Valley has some pretty scary history. Legend has it that gun powder was stored by Union forces in its hollows in the Civil War. They were prepared to blow it up if Confederates crossed over the nearby Meramec River with the idea of capturing St. Louis.

Even scarier is a more recent tale of developers trolling the area with the idea of building a big subdivision. The neighbors protested, the state got involved, and Powder Valley Nature Center was the end result.

While Powder Valley still has fine programs for kids, that Halloween trail has been dropped. What happened? Did the trolls turn to stone?

ROGER PRYOR FOREST

IMAGINE FLOATING IN YOUR CANOE ON A RIVER TWISTING THROUGH A STEEP OZARK CANYON. Night is beginning to fall and things are strangely silent. Suddenly, there is a rustle of trees and plants up ahead. A large creature seems intent on breaking through to the sandbar.

You feel vulnerable. Your canoe party is in a very isolated area. What is it? It is emerging as a large hulk of hillbilly with a flowing beard, long reddish hair and substantial girth. This imposing Big Foot begins to grin at you. Why? Is it because he knows this dense wilderness well, and you've not a clue as to where you are?

The hulking figure in this scary scenario could well have been the late Roger Pryor. I never witnessed Pryor in his favorite backwoods. As a journalist, my experience with Pryor was when he was at a press conference microphone trying to stop another trashing of woods, glade and stream.

Pryor was a pioneer in nature and environmental protection. Indeed, his title was senior environmental policy director with the Missouri Coalition for the Environment. He raised his voice against waste dumps, tailing ponds, forest clear-cutting and more. He was a friend of the forest, so it is appropo that a forest was named for him.

If you've floated the Current River past Round Spring or wound down rural Highway 19 past Round Spring, then you have at least a passing familiarity with the expanse known as Roger Pryor Pioneer Backcountry.

Located in the most remote area of the Ozarks, the 61,000-acre tract is legendary for its solitude, broken only by the occasional backpacker and hiker. The woodland area borders the swift and clear Current River for almost 15 miles—a float stream very often rated as the best in Missouri.

Several rugged trails make their way through this natural refuge. The trail to the Current River Old-Growth Forest offers an acquaintance with trees aged at 400 years and more.

Brushy Creek Trail links to the Laxton Hollow Trail, which connects to a section of the Ozark Trail. Upon completion, the Ozark Trail will wind for several hundred miles through the Ozark Mountains of Missouri and Arkansas. A story in a 1995 edition of *Backpacker Magazine* rated this Pioneer Backcountry trail section as among the ten best Midwest hikes.

Deer, turkey, bats, bobcats, redback salamanders and timber rattlers are in far more abundance than any human specimens here. The dearth of noisy, upright, bipedal humans is a major part of the charm of Pioneer Forest.

When I am at the Pioneer Forest, I imagine Pryor's ghost roaming all about. He's carrying his folk guitar and singing. Nothing scary about this apparition—he wouldn't hurt a flea. A story is told about Pryor. Once bitten by a poisonous snake, he demanded that no one harm his slithering assailant as he was packed off to the hospital.

Route 66 State Park

Take a bike trip through Route 66 State Park. You are riding through an environmental disaster zone—or, at least, what was once a disaster zone. Here sat a town doomed, condemned and eventually destroyed because of a deadly dioxin contamination.

Take a trip through time, and you would find the resort city of Times Beach established here in 1926. Less than 20 miles southwest of St. Louis on the Meramec River, the daily *St. Louis Times* offered beach lots at this site to new subscribers in a "Times Beach" newspaper promotion.

Continue this time machine trip to 1935, and you would find the "Mother Road" of Route 66 tracking through Times Beach. Visitors would find a roadhouse just east of the Meramec River before entering the city.

In the 1970s, you might find a refuse hauler spraying the dirt roads with waste oil to keep the dust down. The oil would be contaminated with dioxin, a byproduct of poisonous defoliants manufactured elsewhere in Missouri for use in the Vietnam War.

In the early 1980s, you would find the city devastated by Meramec River floods. A few years after the flooding, you would witness Environmental Protection Agency workers urging the evacuation of the town, followed by a $32 million federal buyout. Soon, all the residents would be gone.

Take the time machine trip to the 1990s, and you would find a giant incinerator here. It would be burning thousands of tons of soil and debris to neutralize the dioxin from carcinogenic Agent Orange.

Fast-forward to the present. You are now in a pleasant, 419-acre river park. That old roadhouse is a state park museum. There is no sign of the river city of 2,500 once known as Times Beach. It has vanished. There's no trace of the place! Where did it go?

Today's Route 66 State Park is flanked by Ozark foothills, although the park itself is a lazy bicycler's paradise, because its terrain is so flat. That may explain why many visitors prefer to explore the area on two wheels rather than on two legs.

When I'm touring by bike at Route 66, my mind tends to drift—it gets caught up in that time machine. It's a good thing the biking challenge level is low, as well as the need for concentrating on the task at hand. Indeed, there is much to think about on a visit to this setting, which has witnessed so much history, tragedy and change.

Route 66 State Park will forever be Times Beach in my mind. As a journalist, I covered this town's calamity from Washington, D.C., when the federal government tried to ignore the scope of the disaster. Later, I covered the cleanup on-site and watched the huge incinerator belch smoke plumes that frightened residents downwind.

Resting on a park bench here, I think of what my professor once told me. He said: "The war always comes home—even a foreign war." At Times Beach, the Vietnam War came home in the dioxin byproducts of a jungle defoliant.

Shaw Nature Reserve

There's so much to take in at Shaw Nature Reserve. This worthy refuge of the prairie can be overwhelming. A 2,400-acre creation of the world-renowned Missouri Botanical Garden, Shaw is best absorbed in a series of visits spread out over several seasons.

A good place to begin a long-lasting relationship with Shaw is with a jaunt around Pinetum Lake, followed by a prairie hike to the Wetland Trail loop. This long, yet less-than-exhausting excursion can begin at the visitor center. The center is near the main entrance, which is a short drive from the Highway 100 exit off I-44.

The Pinetum (pie-NEE-tum) Lake area consists of conifers—pine, spruce, cedar and fir—cone-bearing beauties that keep Shaw green year-round. Thousands of daffodils bloom in Pinetum's meadows every spring, adding new splashes of floral color among the evergreens.

Before completing the loop around Pinetum Lake, veer off for a prairie hike that begins on the east side of the lake. The prairie hike to the Wetland Trail can be so rewarding in fall and spring, when the wildflower blooms blow with the weather fronts.

The prairie hike takes you to a swinging fence door that is intended to keep the deer from having the run of the place, so be sure to close it behind you. The tall fence serves to let you know you're on the right track and very near the Wetland Trail.

Two features on the Wetland Trail merit your attention. The first is an elevated observation blind. Mounted binoculars in the blind can assist your study of the many birds that thrive on ponds and along the marshes here.

The second feature is the 300-foot boardwalk which hugs the pond area. Walkway benches are just right for a respite from a hike. If you dally long enough, you may become part of the scenery. Red-winged blackbirds may land near you and ask, in their peculiar way, what your intentions are.

Shaw Nature Reserve and its fields full of wildflowers sent me back to the visitor center, which has a treasure trove of information on the blooms of this reclaimed prairie. I picked up the *Prairie Trail Guide* and a wonderful used copy of *The Great Sunflower Book* by Barbara Flores.

Sunflowers abound at Shaw. The towering September sentries known as Maximilians are a wonder. Flores relates how sunflowers were treated as a weed by settlers and farmers. Their beauty and value as a crop were recognized later in the 20th century.

Flores also tells an amazing tale of how sunflowers have been used in the Chernobyl nuclear plant disaster cleanup in the Ukraine. The roots of floating sunflower gardens have been used in contaminated ponds to absorb and isolate the dangerous radionuclides.

In the past, humans have all too casually discarded potential friends in the plant world, dissing them as "just weeds." At Shaw Nature Reserve, humans may shed such prejudices and discover new friends.

Tower Rock

On adventures between St. Louis and Memphis, be advised to consider a detour to pay homage to the "demon that devours travelers." A detour near Cape Girardeau for the demon may eat up some travel time, but it's worth seeing this great natural monument to the travel woes of the past.

Together, these foreboding words, "demon that devours travelers," constitute the name given to Tower Rock by the Shawnee Tribe of Illinois. The missionaries Louis Joliet and Pere Marquette wrote in their journals in 1673 that they were warned about the evil river obstacle by "savages."

The "demon" itself is a giant limestone rock, approximately 80 feet high, that sits in Mississippi waters about 150 feet from the Missouri shore. It's a jagged and eroded layer cake topped with trees and shrubs.

The rock is north of Cape and can be visited on the Missouri side by a gravel road south of the village of Wittenburg. Visitors on the Illinois side should go to the Grand Tower levee or the Devil's Backbone camping park for a good view of the scrubby, shaggy-maned Tower Rock.

Joliet and Marquette were not the only religious to come upon Tower Rock. Father Jean Buisson de Saint Cosme mounted a wooden cross on its summit to dispel the Shawnee belief that evil spirits inhabited the rock.

More French missionaries followed to bring the stories and parables of a new religion to a New World. Some natives became converts. Some listened to the missionaries' holy stories, then offered to tell their own sacred tribal tales and earth myths.

Native Americans were frustrated when the black-collared French missionaries proved uninterested, if not hostile, to their spirit stories. They grew skeptical because of the behavior of Christian settlers and the failure of the missionaries' "magic" to take hold.

With the Tower Rock, the "magic" did not stop river accidents. The turbulent waters and whirlpools around the rock continued to sink boats and take lives. Pirates ravaged and looted settlers who left their keelboats to walk around the river hazard. Evil continued to surround the rock.

Tower Rock became the inspiration for cursing and for taking the name of the Lord in vain. Native Americans were curious that European settlers would insult their God with profane and even sacrilegious speech.

In the mid-1800s, the new breed of Americans contemplated blowing up the rock in a quarry project. Legend has it that President Ulysses S. Grant put a stop to those plans. The rock is now listed on the National Park Service's Register of Historic Places.

Visit Tower Rock. Perhaps you'll curse it as an unnecessary diversion in your travel plans. Or, you may sit and ponder the sunken boats, pirate raids, drowned souls—and come away with respect for Shawnee wisdom and awe for this demon that devours travelers.

DIRECTIONS

UNIQUE BLUFFS & OVERLOOKS

page 7 Arrow Rock is located in Arrow Rock, Mo. From I-70, take Exit 98, Arrow Rock/Pilot Grove. Turn left on Hwy. 41, and head north for 13 miles to Arrow Rock State Historic Site.

The town of Arrow Rock is situated along Arrow Rock Bluff and offers many historic landmarks. The home of artist George Caleb Bingham is on the bluff. Nearby, enjoy picnicking at the 32-acre Boone's Lick State Historic Site, where you can follow an easy trail to the Boone's Lick salt spring.

page 9 Bee Tree Gazebo Overlook, also known as the Chubb Overlook, is located in Bee Tree Park in South St. Louis County. From I-270/255, exit at Telegraph Road and head south. Take a left on Becker Road. Take a left on Finestown Road. Follow to the park. The Chubb Memorial Overlook is located on the bluffs along the Mississippi River.

The park is also home to a seven-acre lake with a fishing dock, and a three-mile hiking trail. Hiking can also be enjoyed at the nearby Cliff Cave Park.

page 11 Benedictine Bluffs are located on the campus of Benedictine College in Atchison, Kan. From I-70, head west toward Kansas. Take Exit 8B to I-435 north toward Des Moines. Follow I-435 north to I-29 north/Hwy. 71 north toward St. Joseph. Take Exit 20 to Hwy. 273. Follow Hwy. 273, then continue right on Hwy. 273/Hwy. 45. Turn left on Hwy. 59. Turn right on South 4th Street. Turn right on Main Street. Main turns into North 2nd Street. Continue to Benedictine College.

The college is situated along the Benedictine Bluffs, which overlook the Missouri River, and can be viewed from Abbey Lookout Point or Ravenswood Overlook.

page 13 Cardareva Bluffs are best enjoyed, and reached, on a canoe trip on the Current River. The bluffs are located just above where Carr Creek enters the river. This is between the Owls Bend Access to the north and the Log Yard Access on the south. The Owls Bend canoe access point is located several miles east of Eminence on Hwy. 106. Eminence can be reached by taking Hwy. 19 south from I-44. The Hwy. 19/Hwy. 106 intersection is at the heart of Eminence.

Intrepid hikers may want to find a way to hike to Cardareva by taking Hwy. 106 beyond Owls Bend. Past Owls Bend, turn south on Rte. HH, which will get travelers to Ozark National Scenic Riverways land just south of Cardareva.

page 15 Castlewood Trail Overlook is located within Castlewood State Park in Ballwin, Mo. From I-44, just west of I-270, take Exit 272/Hwy. 141. Bear right and go north on Hwy. 141. Exit at Big Bend and take a left. Follow through Ballwin for several miles to Ries Road. Turn left on Ries Road and follow into Castlewood State Park.

page 17 Cuivre River Bluffs are located in the Cuivre River State Park in Troy, Mo. From I-70, travel west from St. Louis to Exit 210/Wentzville. Take Hwy. 61 north for 14 miles. Head east on Hwy. 47 to Hwy. 147 at the main entrance to the park.

The park offers scenic woodlands, prairies, ponds and other natural features. Visitors can enjoy hiking, picnicking, camping, fishing and more. A boat launch on Lake Lincoln gives access to small boats.

page 19 Devil's Elbow Bluffs are located four miles west of St. Robert, Mo. From St. Louis, take I-44 west past Rolla to Exit 169, Rte. J. Turn left on J. Then turn right on Rte. Z.

The bluffs overlook the Big Piney River, and canoeists can view the bluffs between Shanghai Spring and the Big Piney's Junction. The Devil's Elbow Bridge also provides views of the bluffs.

page 21 Easley Bluffs are located south of Columbia, Mo., along a bend in the Missouri River known as the Plowboy Bend. The site can be reached by taking I-70 and exiting at Hwy. 63 south, which takes you through Columbia. Once through Columbia, turn right on Hwy. 163. Soon after reaching Rock Bridge State Park, continue straight on Rte. N. Head southwest on Rte. N, which travels all the way to the river and Easley.

Easley also can be reached by bike or a hike on the Katy Trail. It can be found halfway between the stops of McBaine and Hartsburg along the old Katy Railroad, which has now been converted from rail to trail.

page 23 Fults Hill Prairie Bluff is located in Randolph County, Ill. From St. Louis, take I-55 N/I-64 E/I-70 E/Hwy. 40 toward Illinois. Take Hwy. 3 toward Cahokia. Merge onto I-255S/Hwy. 3S toward Columbia. Take a left to continue on Hwy. 3 south toward Columbia. Turn right on Hwy. 3/Great River Road. Follow the Great River Road for approximately 18 miles. Turn left on Shawneetown Trail. Turn right on Hwy. 1/Palestine Road. Turn left on County Lake Road. Turn right to continue on County Lake Road.

The bluffs are located within Fults Hill Prairie State Natural Area. Visitors can enjoy scenic views, hiking and wildlife observation in the natural area.

page 25 Green's Cave Bluff is located within Meramec State Park. From St. Louis, take I-44 west to Exit 266—Sullivan/Hwy. 185. Turn left and go three miles on Hwy. 185. The park entrance is on the right.

The cave can be reached by hiking in from Hwy. 185 or by floating upriver from the Sappington Bridge.

page 27 Ha Ha Tonka Bluffs are located within Ha Ha Tonka State Park. From I-44, take Exit 129 at Lebanon. At the top of the exit, turn to travel north on Hwy. 5 for approximately 30 miles until reaching Camdenton. At the traffic light, turn left onto Hwy. 54 and travel west 2.5 miles before turning left onto Rte. D, which will lead into Ha Ha Tonka State Park.

page 29 Lover's Leap is located in Hannibal, Mo. From St. Louis, take I-70 west to Exit 220, Hwy. 79 north. Follow Hwy. 79 north toward Hannibal. Lover's Leap is located on Hwy. 79 just south of Hannibal. Look for signs to the site.

page 31 Hawn State Bluffs are located along Pickle Creek in Hawn State Park. From St. Louis, take I-55 south to Exit 150, Hwy. 32 west. Follow Hwy. 32 west for 11 miles. Take a left on Hwy. 144 and follow it to Hawn State Park. Pickle Creek can be accessed along the one-mile Pickle Creek Trail or the 10-mile Whispering Pines Trail.

page 33 Hughes Mountain Bluff is located in Hughes Mountain Natural Area, south of Potosi. Take Hwy. 21 eleven miles south of Potosi. Take a left onto Rte. M and follow for five miles. Take a right onto Cedar Creek Road.

page 35 Les Bourgeois Bluffs is located in Rocheport, Mo. From St. Louis, take I-70 west to Exit 115, Rte. BB north toward Rocheport. Turn right onto BB and follow to the Les Bourgeois Winery.

The winery is situated atop the limestone bluffs.

page 37 Lewis and Clark Trail Overlook is part of the Weldon Spring Conservation area on the west side of the Missouri River between Weldon Spring and Defiance. The conservation area can be reached by taking I-64/Hwy. 40 and exiting onto Hwy. 94 south. Drive a bit more than two miles, past Francis Howell High School, until reaching the trailhead to get to the overlook. The trailhead is on the left.

Nearby attractions include the many wineries along Hwy 94 from Defiance to Dutzow. Also nearby is the famous August A. Busch Memorial Conservation Area.

page 39 Little Grand Canyon Bluff is located in the Shawnee National Forest. From St. Louis, take the Dr. Martin Luther King Jr. Memorial Bridge to Hwy. 64 east. Take Exit 50 to Hwy. 127 south. Continue on Hwy. 127 south to Eatherton Road. Head west for five miles and look for signs to the site.

page 41 Park Campus Promontory is located on the campus of Park University in Parkville, Mo. From I-70, head west toward Kansas City. Take Exit 2C to Hwy. 169 north. Turn left onto West 5th Street. Turn right on Hwy. 169 north. Merge onto Hwy. 9 north toward Parkville. End at Park University.

page 43 Pere Marquette Overlook is located in Pere Marquette State Park. From St. Louis, take Hwy. 270 north to Exit 25B, Hwy. 67 north. Follow 67 north toward Alton, and continue to Landmarks Blvd. (still 67 north). Make a slight left onto West Broadway/Hwy. 100/Great River Road. Head north on the Great River Road past Grafton, Ill. The entrance to Pere Marquette State Park is on the right.

page 45 Piasa Bluffs of Elsah are located in Elsah, Ill. From St. Louis, take Hwy. 270 north to Exit 25B, Hwy. 67 north. Follow 67 north toward Alton, and continue to Landmarks Blvd. (still 67 north). Make a slight left onto West Broadway/Hwy.

100/Great River Road. Head north on the Great River Road to Elsah. A painting of the Piasa appears on a bluff wall north of Alton, Ill., on the way to Elsah.

page 47 Pinnacles Ridge is on a tract of land north of Columbia, Mo., known as the Boone County Pinnacles Youth Park. From I-70 in Columbia take either Hwy. 63 or Hwy. 763 north toward Kirksville. Once past the Finger Lakes State Park area and Hwy. 124, look for Pinnacles Road. Take a right onto the Pinnacles Road and travel east to the park entrance and parking lot, which can be found just before Pinnacles Road turns north.

page 49 Rhineland Bluffs are located just west of Rhineland, Mo. From St. Louis, take I-70 west toward Kansas City. Take Hwy. 19 south to Hwy. 94. Turn right and travel west on Hwy. 94 past Rhineland to get to the bluffs.

page 51 Rocheport Bluffs are located in Rocheport, Mo. From St. Louis, take I-70 west to Exit 115, Rte. BB north toward Rocheport. Turn right onto BB, which curves to the Missouri River and Rocheport.

page 53 Sam A. Baker State Park Bluffs are located within Sam A. Baker State Park. From St. Louis, take I-55 south to Exit 174, Hwy. 67. Head south on Hwy. 67 for about 75 miles. Turn right on Hwy. 34 west, and then right on Hwy. 143 and follow to the park.

page 55 Sunset Bluffs are located within Emmenegger Nature Park. From the I-44 and I-270 interchange, take the Watson Road exit and immediately head north on Geyer Road. Take the first left onto Cragwold Drive and follow to the T over the I-270 bridge. Take a left and follow the road to the park entrance, which will be on the right. The bluffs provide views of the Meramec River Valley.

page 57 Trail of Tears Bluffs are located within the Trail of Tears State Park. From St. Louis, take I-55 south to Exit 105 to Hwy. 61 north. Turn right on Hwy. 177, and go about seven miles. You will reach a stop sign near a factory. Continue to the right on Hwy. 177. The park entrance is on the left.

page 59 Truman Lake Bluffs are located within Harry S. Truman State Park in Warsaw, Mo. From I-70, head west to the Sedalia exit. Take Hwy. 65 south to Warsaw. At Warsaw, take Hwy. 7 west. Turn right on Rte. UU and follow to the park.

A variety of activities are offered within the park, including swimming, fishing and hiking. The limestone bluffs overlook the 55,600-acre Truman Lake.

page 61 Vilander Bluffs are located between Onondaga State Park and Meramec State Park on the Meramec River. From I-44, take Exit 214 (Leasburg). Go south on Rte. H for seven miles, passing through the town of Leasburg. The pavement will end at Onondaga State Park. At this point, it is necessary to travel by canoe on the Meramec River to Vilander.

page 63 Washington State Park Overlook is located within Washington State Park. From St. Louis, take Hwy. 21 south through Hillsboro and Desoto. The park is on the right side of the highway about nine miles south of Desoto.

page 65 Weston Bluffs are located within Weston Bend State Park. From Kansas City, take I-29 to Exit 20, Weston/Leavenworth and Atchison, Kan. Take Hwy. 273 west toward Weston. At the intersection of Hwy. 273 and Hwy. 45, turn left and head south. The state park entrance is one half mile on the right.

STREAMS AND SPRINGS

page 71 Alley Spring is located six miles west of Eminence, Mo., on Hwy. 106. From I-44, take Exit 208 to Hwy. 19 south. Follow Hwy. 19 to Hwy. 106 west. Travel five miles to Alley Springs National Park.

Alley Springs has a historic grist mill that is open for daily tours from 9 a.m. to 4 p.m. Memorial Day through Labor Day. Entrance is free, but donations are appreciated. While at the mill, visit the Story Creek Schoolhouse, within walking distance. Eminence is also home to Missouri's only wild horse herds, or you can enjoy canoeing or kayaking the Jacks Fork and Current Rivers.

page 73 Baker/Ozark Dive Rocks are located within Sam A. Baker State Park in Patterson, Mo. From I-55, head south from St. Louis. Take Exit 174, to Hwy. 67 south. Go approximately 75 miles. Turn right/west onto Hwy. 34 and travel five miles. Turn right onto Hwy. 143, which will lead you into Sam A. Baker State Park.

Park amenities and attractions include swimming, fishing, hiking, camping, a nature center and much more.

page 75 Bennett Springs is located in Lebanon, Mo. From I-44, take Exit 129. Turn right at the top of the ramp to Hwy. 5/Hwy. 32. Go 1.5 miles then continue on Hwy. 64 for 10.5 miles. Turn left on Hwy. 64A. Continue to Bennett Springs State Park.

The spring is widely popular for trout fishermen. Park amenities include hiking, camping, canoeing, kayaking, swimming, picnicking and much more. Motel rooms and cabins are also available within the park for a fee. Visit the nature center from 9 a.m. to 5 p.m. daily. The park offers a plethora of wildlife and is thought to be one of the most beautiful parks in Missouri.

page 77 Big Spring is found four miles south of Van Buren on Hwy. 103. Van Buren is located on Hwy. 60 between Sikeston and Springfield in southern Missouri. St. Louis residents can get to Van Buren by taking either I-55 south or Hwy. 67 south, and then turning west on Hwy. 60 to reach Van Buren.

Big Spring is the largest spring in Missouri and one of the largest in the world, pouring out over 278 million gallons of water per day. Visitors to Big Spring can enjoy hiking, camping and picnicking. The beautiful nearby Mark Twain National Forest offers a variety of recreational activities for the nature lover. The Current and Jacks Fork rivers boast some of the best float trips in Missouri.

page 79 Blue Spring is located 12 miles east of Eminence, Mo., on Hwy. 106. From I-44, take Exit 208 to Hwy. 19 south. Follow Hwy. 19 to Hwy. 106 east. Follow to Blue Spring Natural Area.

There is a quarter-mile walk to the spring from the parking area. While in the area, be sure to visit Rocky Falls Shut-ins, one of Missouri's most beautiful geological features, or relax and enjoy a canoe trip on the nearby Current River.

page 81 Castor River Shut-ins is located within the Amidon Conservation Area about eight miles east of Fredericktown, Mo. From I-55 south, take Exit 174B to Hwy. 67 south. Follow 67 to Hwy. 72 and head east. Or, from I-55 north, take Exit 99 to Business I-55, then follow to Hwy. 72 west toward Fredericktown. From either side, follow 72 to Rte. J. Go north on Rte. J for 4.4 miles to Rte. W. Turn right on W. Rte. W will turn from blacktop to gravel. At this point you are now on Madison Hwy. 208. At the fork in the road, turn left and go .9 miles to parking area. When you get to the fork in the road, stop and get an area map there.

Take the Cedar Glade Trail to view the shut-ins, as well as two abandoned mills. While visiting the shut-ins, consider a dip in the pool below the last set of falls.

page 83 Chain of Rocks, known as Chain of Rocks Bridge, is a bikeway that connects the cities of St. Louis and Granite City, Ill. From Missouri (St. Louis County), take I-270 east and exit at Riverview Drive south. The entrance is on the left. (St. Louis City) Take I-55/70, exit at Adelaide, go right to Hall Street, then left to Riverview Drive. Entrance is just before intersection of I-270 and Riverview. From Illinois, take I-270 west, Exit Hwy. 3 south, then head west on Old Chain of Rocks Road. Parking can be found along Riverview Drive in St. Louis near the Route 66 Bikeway Entrance.

The bridge can be walked or biked and offers outstanding views of the St. Louis skyline and the Mississippi River. Bald eagles may also be seen during winter months. Two structures that once served as water intakes are also visible. Just south of the Chain of Rocks, you can pick up the St. Louis Riverfront Trail, which runs from the North Riverfront Park to the Gateway Arch.

page 85 Creve Coeur Lake is located in Maryland Heights, Mo., just west of St. Louis. From I-270, exit at I-70 and go west. From I-70, take Exit 231, Earth City Expressway. Follow Earth City Expressway south to its end, turn right at Maryland Heights Expressway Road, go about one mile, and turn left onto Marine Drive. Proceed on Marine Drive about a quarter of a mile to the Sailboat Cove entry to Creve Coeur Park. The park can also be accessed by heading west on Dorsett Road off I-270, just north of the new Page Expressway.

As you enter the Sailboat Cove parking area, you will see the boathouse about 150 yards off to your right across a field. There's an access road leading from the boathouse. Fishing and non-gasoline boats are permitted on the lake. Swimming is not allowed. While at the lake, Creve Coeur Park offers a variety of activities including disc golf, archery, athletic fields, tennis courts, playgrounds and picnicking, and the beautiful "dripping springs" waterfall makes for a popular wedding spot. The park is well known for its paved walking and cycling trail.

page 87 Grand Falls is located in Joplin, Mo. From I-44, take Exit 6 to Hwy. 86 south. Go about one mile south and cross Shoal Creek. After crossing the bridge, turn right. Follow the road along the creek for three miles. The falls are on the right.

The Grand Falls flows year-round and visitors can view the falls from the many rock formations along the creek.

page 89 Gravois Creek/Grant's Trail is located in St. Louis, providing a paved trail that currently runs approximately eight miles through St. Louis County, between I-55 and I-44. Several access points are available.

Orlando Gardens parking—Take I-55 to Union Road exit and go left. Take a left on Leeshore, left on Friartuck and a right on Hoffmeister. The trail begins at the east end of the parking lot of Orlando Gardens Banquet Center.

Watson Road parking—From the east, take I-44 to Exit 280, Elm Ave. Go south on Elm to Watson Road. Go right on Watson. At the second traffic light, there is a strip mall on the right. The trail is just east of the stoplight. From the west, take I-270 to I-44 east/Watson exit and stay right to go onto Watson. Head east on Watson for about 2.25 miles. Look for the strip mall on the left, at the bottom of the hill after passing Westfield Crestwood Mall. The trail is just east of the stoplight.

The trail runs parallel to Gravois Creek. Visitors can walk, inline skate, or bike the six-plus miles of trail. Long-term plans are to extend the trail. Nearby Grant's Farm, at mile-marker five from the east, offers visitors a chance to see the 281-acre farm operated by Anheuser-Busch, Inc. The farm is home to over 1,000 animals that can be viewed by a guided tram ride. The farm also houses the famous Anheuser-Busch Clydesdales. Children can feed baby goats and see hundreds of other animals, or enjoy an educational animal show in the Tier Garten. Adults can try complimentary samplings of Anheuser-Busch products in the hospitality room. Food and beverages are available to all in the courtyard. Admission is free and there is parking for a fee.

page 91 Greer Spring is located 18 miles south of Winona on Hwy. 19. From I-55 near Sikeston, take Exit 66B to Hwy. 60 west. Continue on 60 west about 52 miles. Merge to 60 west toward Springfield, continue about 4.5 miles. Merge to 60 west toward Van Buren and continue about 57 miles. Turn left on Hwy. 19 headed south. From I-44, take Exit 82A to Hwy. 65 south toward Branson. Merge onto Hwy. 60 East toward Cabool. Continue to merge on Hwy. 60 east. Turn right on Hwy. 19 south. There will be a sign for the trailhead to Greer Springs and a parking area. There is a one-mile hiking trail to the spring. Campgrounds are also available. The Forest Services Office of Winona lies just north of Hwy. 60, on Hwy. 19. The office can provide additional information and area maps.

Nearby Mark Twain National Forest provides hundreds of miles of hiking trails, over 350-miles of beautiful streams, and is popular with hunters, fishermen and photographers.

page 93 Ha Ha Tonka Spring is located within Ha Ha Tonka State Park. From I-44, take Exit 129 at Lebanon, Mo. At the top of the exit, turn to travel north on Hwy. 5 for approximately 30 miles until Camdenton. At the traffic light, turn left onto Hwy. 54 and travel west 2.5 miles before turning left onto Rte. D, which will lead into Ha Ha Tonka State Park. From I-70, take Exit 148 at Kingdom City. Turn left and head west on Hwy. 54 for approximately 86 miles until reaching Camdenton. You'll pass through Jefferson City and Osage Beach. From the traffic light in Camdenton, continue on Hwy. 54 for 2.5 miles before turning left onto Rte. D, which will lead into Ha Ha Tonka State Park.

Situated in Ha Ha Tonka State Park, the spring is Missouri's twelfth largest. Visitors to the park will find over 15 miles of scenic hiking trails that lead to caves, sinkholes, bluffs, a natural bridge, and even the ruins of an old castle. Fishing is not permitted in the spring but is allowed at the access points to the Lake of the Ozarks.

page 95 Jacks Fork Hideaway is located on the Jacks Fork River between Alley Springs and Eminence, Mo. Alley Spring is located six miles west of Eminence on Hwy. 106. From I-44, take Exit 208 to Hwy. 19 south. Follow Hwy. 19 to Hwy. 106 west. Travel five miles to Alley Springs National Park.

page 97 Jonhson's Shut-ins is approximately 130 miles from St. Louis. Take I-55 south to Hwy. 67 south to Farmington. At the second Farmington exit, turn right onto Rte. W toward Doe Run. Travel 17 miles on Rte. W. At the flashing red light, turn right/north onto Hwy. 21. Travel about one-half mile and turn left onto Rte. N. Go 13 miles on Rte. N to the park entrance on your left.

A quarter-mile walkway will take you to an observation deck overlooking the shut-ins. interpretive sites, picnic tables, a playground and a park store are available. Swimming is not permitted in the shut-ins or any part of the East Fork of the Black River within the park boundaries. Elephant Rocks State Park, just north on Hwy. 21 boasts massive granite boulders that provide a fun atmosphere where visitors can meander along the Braille Trail or climb freely through the maze of these giant rocks.

page 99 Maramec Spring is located eight miles southeast of St. James, Mo., on Hwy. 8. From St. Louis, take I-44 west to Exit 195, St. James. Take Hwy. 8 east of St. James. The entrance to the park is clearly marked.

Maramec Spring is the main attraction of the park and is open to trout fishing. Feed machines are located on the trails for guests to feed the fish. Besides trout fishing, Maramec Spring Park has a reception center, cafe, campground, picnic areas, museums, playgrounds, trails, tennis courts and the historic ironworks. Located at the west end of the park, take the time to travel the historic drive for scenic views of the Meramec River Valley, as well as historic landmarks along the way.

page 101 Mina Sauk Falls are located within Taum Sauk Mountain State Park approximately 120 miles from St. Louis. Take I-55 south to Hwy. 67 south to Farmington. At the 2nd Farmington exit, turn right onto Rte. W. Go 17 miles on Rte. W. At the flashing red light, continue through heading south on Hwy. 21. Go nine miles south on Hwy. 21 until you come to Rte. CC. Turn right onto Rte. CC. Travel about five miles to the state park.

The three-mile Mina Sauk Falls Trail will lead you to the falls. A section of this trail makes up the Taum Sauk portion of the Ozark Trail. While at the park, you can continue about 13 miles on the Ozark Trail to nearby Johnson's Shuts-ins State

Park. Other attractions in the local area include Elephants Rocks State Park and Fort Davidson State Historic Site.

page 103 Roaring River Spring is located in Cassville, Mo., within Roaring River State Park. From I-44, head west toward Springfield. Take Exit 46 to the I-44 Business Loop. Turn left onto the Business Loop. Continue to follow Hwy. 265/Hwy. 39. Turn right on Hwy. 39. Turn right on Hwy. 248. Turn left on Hwy. 112. Take a slight left on Hwy. 112 spur. Follow to Roaring River State Park.

The Nature Center is open from March to October, 9 a.m. to 5 p.m., and offers information about the park's history. The park offers fishing, camping, hiking, picnicking and swimming. Table Rock State Park, nearby in Branson, allows access to Table Rock Lake, where water enthusiasts can rent boats, fish, scuba dive, swim or parasail.

page 105 Round Spring is located north of Eminence, Mo. From I-44, take Exit 208 to Hwy. 19 south. Follow 19 south for about 65 miles. Round Spring is south of Salem about 13 miles north of Eminence on Hwy. 19.

Round Spring flows into the Current River, where canoe enthusiasts can begin an 18-mile float to Twin Rivers. Nearby Round Spring Caverns offers lantern tours for groups of 15 people from 10 a.m. to 2 p.m. daily.

page 107 Rocky Falls is located near Eminence, Mo. From I-44, take Exit 208 to Hwy. 19 south toward Cuba. Follow Hwy. 19 south to Hwy. 106 east. Follow 106 east to Rte. H. Head south on H. Turn onto Rte. NN. Take the second gravel road to the right and follow the signs.

Rocky Falls has a parking area for visitors. Views of the waterfall, swimming, picnicking and hiking can all be enjoyed at the falls. Nearby, Round Spring is a great place to start a float trip or explore the Round Spring Caverns.

page 109 Springfield Refuge is located southeast of Springfield, Mo. From I-44, head west toward Springfield. Take Exit 82A onto Hwy. 65 south. Continue south and merge onto Hwy. 60 west. Follow 60 west and take the Hwy. 65/Glenstone exit and turn left toward Republic Road. Then turn left onto Glenstone Ave. Turn right onto S. Chrisman Ave., which dead ends at the Springfield Conservation Nature Center, which this book refers to as Springfield Refuge.

The center offers a natural history museum and over 80-acres of hiking trails. The center is open year-round from 8 a.m. to 5 p.m. Nearby, visitors can enjoy walking, hiking and biking on the miles of trails of the Ozark Greenways.

CAVES AND CAVERNS

page 115 Bonne Terre Underground Mines is located 60 miles south of St. Louis, in southeast Missouri. From I-55, take Exit 174B to Hwy. 67 south toward Bonne Terre. Exit onto Hwy. 47/Rte. K and head south. Continue on Benham Street. Go left on North Allen Street. Bonne Terre Mines Inc. is located at 39 N. Allen Street.

Parking is free. Scuba-diving tours are available for a fee through West End

Diving, located in Bridgeton, Mo. Walking and boating tours run every hour. If time allows, nearby St. Francois State Park offers the pristine waters of Booneville Creek, abundant camping and access to the Big River, ideal for canoeing and kayaking.

page 117 Bridal Cave is located in central Missouri in the Lake of the Ozarks region. From I-44, take Exit 135 to Rte. F and take a right. Turn right on Hwy. 5. Bridal Cave is located on Lake Road 5-88 at 526 Bridal Cave Road. The cave is also accessible by boat, located at the 10-mile marker of the Big Niangua Arm of the Lake of the Ozarks.

Guided tours run daily for a fee. The two-hour discovery tour, which includes Bridal Cave, Thunder Mountain and Bear Cave, can also be booked for a fee. The cave can be reserved for wedding ceremonies. Be sure to check out the nearby Thunder Mountain Park, where you can take in views of the rocky bluffs and abundant native wildlife on the Thunder Mountain Nature Trail.

page 119 Cathedral Cave is located in Onondaga Cave State Park approximately 90 miles from downtown St. Louis. From I-44, take Exit 214 (Leasburg). Go south on Rte. H for seven miles, passing through the town of Leasburg. The pavement will end at Onondaga State Park. Be sure not to cross the Meramec River.

Lantern tours are offered on Saturdays and Sundays for a fee. While in the park, tours of the Onondaga Cave are also available for a fee. Nearby Meramec State Park also offers cave tours, as well as stunning views of the Meramec River Valley and various outdoor activities.

page 121 Cliff Cave is located south of St. Louis along the Mississippi River. From I-270/255, exit at Telegraph Road and head south. Take a left on Cliff Cave Road, directly across from Baumgartner Road. Follow into Cliff Cave Park Road, which dead ends at the railroad tracks. Trailheads can be accessed from the paved road.

Cliff Cave itself may only be explored by permit, available through the St. Louis County Department of Parks and Recreation. However, numerous trails wind throughout the park, accessible without permit by foot, bike or horseback. To complete your day, head just north to Jefferson Barracks Park, where you can walk, bike or skate the miles of paved trails, try your hand at disc golf, or visit one of the historic museums.

page 123 Crystal Cave is located five miles north of Springfield, Mo. From I-44, take Exit 80B to Rte. H. Go north on H to the intersection of H and KK. Turn left and then immediately on your right is Crystal Cave.

Guided tours run daily for a fee. If time allows, visit nearby Fellows Lake Recreation Area, a popular spot among the locals for fishing and boating.

page 125 Devil's Icebox is located in Rock Bridge State Park, south of Columbia in central Missouri. From I-70 exit onto 163 south, which takes you through Columbia. Once out of Columbia, begin looking for signs that direct you to take a left turn to the state park. If you find yourself heading west on Rte. K to McBaine, you have missed the turn and you are traveling west toward the Missouri River and the Katy Trail.

At Rock Bridge Park, you will find a trail from the parking lot that takes you to the Rock Bridge, which you can walk over or under to get to the Devil's Icebox farther down the boardwalk trail. Other attractions within a few miles of Rock Bridge and the Devil's Icebox are Eagles Bluffs Conservation Area, the Katy Trail to the west and Three Creeks Conservation Area to the southeast.

page 127 Fantastic Caverns is located in Springfield, Mo. From I-44, take Exit 77 to Hwy. 13 and head north. Follow the signs to the Fantastic Caverns.

The caverns are open to tours year-round for a fee. Tours are by guided tram only, making this cave accessible to small children, handicapped and elderly visitors. While in the area, take in over 170 species of wild animals with a train ride through Springfield's Dickerson Park Zoo, or enjoy free conservational education activities at the Springfield Conservation Nature Center.

page 129 Fisher Cave is located in Meramec State Park in Sullivan, Mo. From I-44, take Exit 226 to Hwy. 185 south. Follow Hwy. 185 south for three miles. The park entrance is on the right.

Tours of Fisher Cave are run seasonally for a small fee. Your sightseeing wouldn't be complete without a trip to nearby Onondaga State Park, home of Cathedral and Onondaga caves, as well as the Vilander Bluff Natural Area, which offers scenic views of the Meramec River Valley.

page 131 Graham Cave is located in Graham Cave State Park near Danville, Mo. From I-70, take Exit 170 Danville/Montgomery City. Coming from the west, take a left then an immediate left again onto Rte. TT. From the east, take a right, then an immediate left onto Rte. TT. Continue on Rte. TT into the state park.

Visitors must check in at the park office where maps of the cave are available. This shallow cave allows for a self-guided tour. While at the park, enjoy several hiking trails through the 350-plus acres of diverse terrain or spend the day fishing and boating on the Loutre River. The park also offers wooded campsites for those looking to spend more than a day in the park.

page 133 Jacob's Cave is located north of the Lake of the Ozarks, just south of Versailles, Mo. From I-44, take Exit 129 to Hwy. 32/Hwy. 5 toward Lebanon/Hartville. Travel north on Hwy. 5 for approximately 55 miles. Go right on Rte. TT. End at Jacob's Cave.

Tours run seasonally for a fee, and Jacob's Cave is the only walking tour that is completely handicapped accessible. With over 1,300 miles of beautiful shoreline, the Lake of the Ozarks is a must-see for all visitors to the area.

page 135 Mark Twain Cave is located in Hannibal, Mo. From Hwy. 61, take I-72E/Hwy. 32E/61-BR E. Merge onto Hwy. 79 south via Exit 157. Turn right on Fulton Avenue to the Mark Twain Cave.

Guided tours run daily for a fee. Camping is available for those staying overnight. Spend the day in historic Hannibal, Mo., the boyhood home of Samuel Clemens. While there, be sure to see the Mark Twain Boyhood Home, the Becky

Thatcher House and a variety of shops, restaurants and other attractions that adorn the main streets.

page 137 Marvel Cave is located within Silver Dollar City Theme Park, in Branson, Mo. From I-44, take the Hwy. 65 south Exit 82A to Branson. Take the Hwy. 248/Hwy. 65-BR ramp to Shepherd of the Hills Expwy. Turn right at Red Route. Turn right at Hwy. 265. Turn left at Stormy Point Road. Continue on Showplace Gtwy. Turn right at Timberlane Point Road. Arrive at Silver Dollar City.

Cave tours are included in the entrance fee to the Silver Dollar City Theme Park. While in Branson, hop aboard the Showboat Branson Belle for a scenic tour of Table Rock Lake or take part in some of Missouri's best freshwater fishing in nearby Table Rock Lake.

page 139 Meramec Caverns is located about 60 miles west of St. Louis in Stanton, Mo. From I-44, take Exit 230 Stanton and follow the signs to the caverns.

Tours run daily for a fee and the caverns are handicapped accessible. While visiting the caverns, tours aboard the Cavern Queen offer a scenic riverboat ride down the Meramec River. Canoes and rafts are available to rent for float trips. Overnighters can enjoy camping or a stay in the Meramec Caverns Motel. Be sure to also visit nearby Meramec State Park.

page 141 Onondaga Cave is located in Onondaga Cave State Park approximately 90 miles from downtown St. Louis. From I-44, take Exit 214 (Leasburg). Go south on Rte. H for seven miles, passing through the town of Leasburg. The pavement will end at Onondaga State Park. Be sure not to cross the Meramec River.

Walking tours are available year-round for a fee. While in the park, tours of the Cathedral Cave are also available for a fee. There is plenty to do at nearby Meramec State Park, such as fishing, hiking, floating and camping.

page 143 Ozark Cave is located south of the Grand Glaize arm of the Lake of the Ozarks. From I-70, take Exit 148 at Kingdom City. Turn left and head south and west on Hwy. 54 through Jefferson City and Osage Beach. A couple miles south of Grand Glaize Bridge, turn left and head west on Rte. A. Look for signs for Ozark Caverns and turn left on a road that dead-ends near the cave site.

Tours run April through October for a fee. There are three types of tours to choose from. Lake of the Ozarks State Park's main area, located north of the Grand Glaize arm of the Lake of the Ozarks, offers numerous recreational activities for all ages. The unspoiled beauty of the park's many trails can be explored by foot, horseback and bicycle, and the water can be enjoyed by boat or from one of the park's two beaches. Over 200 campgrounds are available to the overnight guests of the park.

page 145 River Cave is located in Ha Ha Tonka State Park. From I-44, take Exit 129 at Lebanon. At the top of the exit, turn right and travel north on Hwy. 5 for approximately 30 miles until Camdenton. At the traffic light, turn left onto Hwy. 54 and travel west 2.5 miles before turning left onto Rte. D, which will lead into Ha Ha Tonka State Park. From I-70, take Exit 148 at Kingdom City. Turn left and head west on Hwy. 54 for approximately 86 miles until reaching Camdenton. From the traffic light in Camdenton, continue on Hwy. 54 for 2.5 miles before turning left onto Rte. D, which will lead into Ha Ha Tonka State Park.

Located at the bottom of a sinkhole, a staircase leads you down to River Cave. The park features bluffs, caves and other geologic features, as well as fifteen miles of hiking trails.

page 147 Rock Bridge is located in Rock Bridge State Park, south of Columbia in central Missouri. From I-70 exit onto 163 south, which takes you through Columbia. Once out of Columbia, begin looking for signs that direct you to take a left turn to the state park. If you find yourself heading west on Rte. K to McBaine, you have missed the turn and you are traveling west toward the Missouri River and the Katy Trail.

Nearby Finger Lakes State Park offers ATV trails, mountain biking and motocross tracks, as well as numerous other recreational activities.

page 149 Round Spring Cave is located off Hwy. 19, north of Eminence, Mo. From I-44, take Exit 208 to Hwy. 19 south. Follow 19 south for about 65 miles. Round Spring is about 13 miles north of Eminence on Hwy. 19.

Guided lantern tours run Memorial Day through Labor Day for a fee. Eminence provides access to the Jacks Fork and Current rivers, both perfect settings for canoeing, kayaking, fishing and swimming. The nearby Rocky Falls Shut-ins displays a beautiful cascading waterfall and pristine swimming hole.

page 151 Talking Rocks is conveniently located just minutes west of Silver Dollar City and Branson, Mo. From I-44, take the Hwy. 65 south Exit 82A to Branson. Take the Hwy. 465/Rte. F. Turn right at Ozark Mountain Highroad. Turn left at Hwy. 76. Bear right at Hwy. 76. Turn left at Hwy. 13. Turn left at 13-280/Talking Rocks Road. Turn right at Fairy Cave Lane. Arrive at Talking Rocks Cavern.

Daily tours of the cavern are available for a fee and run year-round. Nearby Table Rock Lake is a blue water paradise for boaters, fisherman and campers. Many resorts line the lake and provide endless activities for all ages.

page 153 Vineyard Cave is located in Ste. Genevieve, Mo. On I-55, head south of St. Louis to Exit 150. Head west on Hwy. 32. Take a left on Rte. B. Travel six miles and take a left on Rte. P. Follow Rte. P for two miles. Take a right on Cave Road. Follow Cave Road for two miles to Vineyard Cave.

There is a short walk to the cave where visitors can enjoy a picnic lunch. Above the cave is the wine-tasting room and gift shop.

JUST SPECIAL PLACES

page 159 Allred Lake Cypress Swamp is located 15 miles south of Poplar Bluff in southeast Missouri. From St. Louis, take I-55 south to Exit 66B to Hwy. 60 west. Head west for 50-plus miles to Hwy. 67 south. Turn left on Hwy. 142, and continue on Rte. HH. Turn right on Rte. H for 2.5 miles to the southbound gravel road, which will take you to the Allred Lake Natural Area.

Amenities and activities include a viewing platform on the lake's west side; hiking, bird watching, and picnicking. The nearby Poplar Bluff section of the Mark Twain National Forest offers two recreational areas with fishing, boating, hiking, and horseback riding.

page 161 Big Oak Tree State Park is located in southeast Missouri. From St. Louis take I-55 to Exit 58 to Hwy. 80 east. Take Hwy. 80 through East Prairie to Hwy. 102 south. Follow Hwy. 102 to Big Oak Tree State Park.

Amenities and activities include a boardwalk through the park, an interpretive center, numerous shelters and tables for picnicking, and the 22-acre Big Oak Lake is stocked with crappie, bass, bluegill, and catfish and is open year-round with boat access. Morris State Park is nearby with hiking that features rare plant species and Crowley's Ridge, towering over 200 feet above the Mississippi River Valley.

page 163 Blue River Parkway is located along the Blue River just south of Kansas City. From I-70, take Exit 15A to I-470 south. Then take Exit 1A to Hwy. 71 south. Exit to Hwy. 150 and head west. Take the Holmes Road/Rte. D ramp and go left. Turn right on Kenneth Road.

Directions to the main trailhead: At the south end of the I-435 loop, take I-435 (east/west) to the Holmes Road exit. Go south on Holmes to 117th Terrace. Take a left onto 117th Terrace and follow it one block until it ends at Troost. Take a right onto Troost, then take the first left onto 118th Street. Follow 118th Street across the railroad bridge to the trailhead.

Alternate trailhead in Minor Park: At the south end of the I-435 loop, take I-435 (east/west) to the Holmes Road exit. Go south on Holmes to Red Bridge Road. Go left on Red Bridge, across the bridge. The park entrance is the first right just past the bridge. Park at the south end of the road.

The park offers trails that can accommodate mountain bikers and horseback riders in some parts. The park also has softball, soccer and polo fields, picnic areas, and areas to fly radio-controlled airplanes. Nearby Minor Park is home to some of the most impressive and well-preserved Sante Fe Trail wagon swales in the Midwest. A hiking trail, 18-hole public golf course and a driving range can be found here as well.

page 165 Butterfly Garden is located on Washington University's Danforth Campus in St. Louis. From I-64/40 take Exit 33B to Big Bend and head north. Follow Big Bend to Forsyth and make a right. The gardens are on the south side of the street across from the parking garage. The garden is outdoor and open to the public.

Forest Park, St. Louis's largest park and one of the largest city parks in the country, is just east of Washington University. Visitors can spend the day wandering through the Saint Louis Zoo, enjoying paddle boating on the Great Basin, seeing hundreds of permanent floral displays in the Jewel Box or climbing on the concrete turtles in the Turtle Playground.

page 167 Chubb Trail is located just west of St. Louis and runs from West Tyson County Park through Castlewood State Park and into Lone Elk County Park. To access the trail from West Tyson County Park, take I-44, just west of I-270, to Exit 266/Lewis Road. Turn right onto Lewis Road. Bear left onto North Outer Road. Enter the park on your right.

To access the trail from Lone Elk County Park, take I-44, just west of I-270, to Exit 272/Hwy. 141. Follow the exit to the top and bear right. Immediately on the right you will see signs for the park. Take your first right toward the Outer Road. At the bottom of the ramp, go left on Meramec Street, which becomes West Outer Road. Follow the Outer Road to the park's entrance.

To access the trail from Castlewood State Park, take I-44, just west of I-270, to Exit 272/Hwy. 141. Bear right and go north on Hwy. 141. Exit at Big Bend and take a left. Follow through Ballwin for several miles to Ries Road. Turn right on Ries Road and follow into Castlewood State Park.

No fee is required at any of the parks. The trail is approximately seven miles and begins near the Chubb Shelter in West Tyson County Park. It ends at the entrance to Lone Elk County Park. The trail is open to hikers and mountain bikers. Lone Elk County Park offers a scenic loop that gives visitors a chance to see herds of elk, deer and bison, as well as wild turkey and waterfowl. The park has multiple picnic areas and trails for hiking.

page 169 Claire Gempp Davidson Conservation Area is located in Sunset Hills, Mo. From I-270, take Exit 3 to Gravois/Hwy. 30. Head east on Gravois. Take a left on Sappington Road. The park is between Gravois and Eddie and Park Road.

The area has a parking lot and is open to the public. Nearby Grant's Farm is a great place for families to spend the day.

page 171 Creve Coeur Wetlands is located southwest of Creve Coeur Lake and is unofficially known as Little Creve Coeur Lake. From I-270, take Exit 616A to Page/364 and head west. Go right on Creve Coeur Mill Road.

The wetlands have a bike trail, and birders are welcome. Nearby Creve Coeur Park offers several recreational activities for all ages, including fishing, hiking and picnicking.

page 173 Devil's Tollgate is located within Taum Sauk Mountain State Park in the St. Francois Mountains. From St. Louis, take I-55 south to Hwy. 67 south toward Farmington. Take the second Farmington exit and turn right on Rte. W, toward Doe Run. Go 17 miles on Rte. W. You will pass through a flashing red light. Continue on Hwy. 21 for nine miles. Turn right on Rte. CC. Follow CC to the park.

Devil's Tollgate is in the Taum Sauk section of the Ozark trail, one mile below the Mina Sauk Falls. The park provides a glimpse into some of Missouri's best-preserved natural areas, giving visitors unmatched solitude for hiking and other activities. The 7,448-acre park boasts the highest peak in Missouri, Taum Sauk Mountain, at 1,772 feet. The highest point can be easily accessed from the parking area.

page 175 Elephant Rocks, or Elephant Rocks State Park, is located southwest of St. Louis. Take I-55 to Exit 174/Hwy. 67. Follow Hwy. 67 south into Farmington. Exit to Rte. W. Follow W for 18 miles to a flashing red light. Turn right onto Hwy. 21 north. The park is about two miles on the right.

The one-mile Braille Trail gives park visitors easy access to the giant granite boulders known as the elephant rocks. Nearby Fort Davidson Historic site takes you back in time to the Pilot Knob Battlefield. The visitor's center has numerous exhibits pertaining to the battle, and a picnic area and playground provide an area for families to enjoy the park setting.

page 177 Russell E. Emmenegger Nature Park from the I-44 and I-270 interchange, take the Watson Road exit and immediately head north on Geyer Road. Take the first left onto Cragwold Drive and follow to the T, over the I-270 bridge. Take a left and follow the road to the park entrance, which will be on the right.

The park offers 1.5 miles of hiking trails, picnic areas and a shelter. The park sits along the Meramec River where visitors can fish, canoe and kayak. Nearby Powder Valley Nature Center conducts nature programs that take visitors into Emmenegger Park. Powder Valley is also a great place to spend the day hiking and enjoying nature.

page 179 Grand Gulf is located 12 miles from the Arkansas border, in Thayer, Mo. From I-44, head west toward Rolla. Take Exit 186, I-44-LOOP/Hwy. 63/Hwy. 72 toward Rolla. Turn Left onto I-44 BL W/Hwy. 63 S/Hwy. 72 S/N Bishop Ave. Continue to follow Hwy. 63 south. Turn right on Rte. F. Turn left on Hwy. 377, Stay straight to Hwy. 377. Turn right on Rte. W. Follow to the park.

Four platforms can be accessed from a quarter-mile boardwalk providing views of the Grand Gulf. One hundred and eighteen stairs lead to the bottom of the Gulf and can be reached from the parking lot. Just south over the Arkansas border, visit Mammoth Spring State Park, featuring a scenic 10-acre lake, picnic areas, a hiking trail, playgrounds and other features.

page 181 Kansas City Glades, or Blue River Glades Natural Area, is located just south of Swope Park in Kansas City. From I-70, take Exit 8a to I-435 south toward Wichita. Take Exit 66 to Hwy. 350E to 63rd/Lee's Summit. Merge onto East 63rd Street. Right onto East 63rd Street TRFY. U-turn at Lewis Road. From Swope Park head a mile south on Blue River Road to the Blue River Glades Natural Area.

page 183 Knob Noster's great tree forest is located within Knob Noster State Park, near Sedalia, Mo. From I-70, head west toward Kansas City. Take Exit 58 to Hwy. 23 south toward Waverly. Turn left on Hwy. 23/N. Main Street. Turn right on SE 10 Road. Follow to Knob Noster State Park.

Several trails are open to hikers, bikers and horseback. Wooded campgrounds are available, and fishing can be enjoyed in one of the park's two lakes.

page 185 Mastadon State Park is located south of St. Louis, in Imperial, Mo. From I-55, take Exit 186 to Imperial/Kimmswick. Go west on Imperial Main Street. Turn right onto West Outer 55. Turn left onto Seckman Road to enter the picnic area or turn left on Museum Drive to get to the museum entrance.

Mastadon State Park contains an archeological and paleontological site. A picnic area, campsites and hiking trails are available to visitors of the park. The museum presents a slideshow, and there is an entrance fee for adults.

page 187 Pickle Springs is located near Farmington, Mo. From I-55, take Exit 150 near Ste. Genevieve to Hwy. 32 west. Follow Hwy. 32 to Rte. AA. Take Rte. AA one mile to Dorlac Road. Follow about a half mile to the parking lot and trailhead.

Pickle Springs Natural Area features a two-mile trail that takes hikers through the many geologic features. The area is open from 4 a.m. to 10 p.m. daily. A visit to nearby Hawn State Park offers a beautiful short hike along the Pickle Creek and a peek at the area's unique sandstone landscape. The park has two longer hikes that offer magnificent views and are very popular amongst backpackers.

page 189 Powder Valley Nature Center is located just west of St. Louis in Kirkwood, Mo. From the intersection of I-270 and I-44, take the Watson Road ramp and follow to the first traffic light. Take a left on Geyer Road. Take a left on Cragwold Road and follow to the nature center.

The Powder Valley Nature Center is open daily from 8 a.m. to 5 p.m. The center is home to several nature exhibits, including a 3,000-gallon freshwater aquarium. A library in the center is open to the public. Three miles of paved trails take you through the park's 112 acres of forest. A few miles farther west on I-44, Lone Elk County Park is home to herds of elk, bison and deer that can be viewed along a paved road that meanders through the park.

page 191 Roger Pryor Forest is located south of Salem, Mo., on Hwy. 19. From I-44, take Exit 208 to Hwy. 19 south. Follow 19 south past Round Spring. The forest is located roughly between Round Spring and Eminence. You will see signs marking the forest.

The backcountry can be accessed from several designated hiking trails, including the Himont Connector Trail and the Brushy Creek Trail.

page 193 Route 66 State Park is located in Eureka, Mo. From I-44, take Exit 266 to Lewis Road. Follow Lewis Road north and curve to the left. Pass West Tyson County Park. You will enter the park just past the visitor's center.

Ample parking is available, and trailheads are clearly marked. Paved trails are open to pedestrians, bikes and horses. A boat ramp allows river access. The visitor's center is open 9:00 a.m. to 4:30 p.m. daily. Historic Route 66 memorabilia are on display. Nearby Castlewood State Park offers a variety of outdoor opportunities, such as hiking, mountain biking, fishing, kayaking and canoeing. The sprawling grassy fields are perfect for picnicking. Terrific views of the Meramec River can be captured along the River Scene Trail.

page 195 Shaw Nature Reserve is located in Gray Summit, Mo. From I-44, take Exit 253/Gray Summit. Head south from the exit and turn right at the intersection. Go 50 yards to the iron gates on the left.

The visitor's center is located near the entrance and has interpretive displays and information about the reserve. The grounds are open 7 a.m. to sunset. An entrance fee is required. Fourteen miles of hiking trails take you throughout the reserve. Several historic buildings are open to the public.

Purina Farms, also located in Gray Summit, is a great way for the animal-lover to spend a day. The relationship between human and pet is displayed through the many exhibits, shows, demonstrations and hands-on activities.

page 197 Tower Rock is located about 10 miles east of Uniontown in southeast Missouri. Uniontown is halfway between Perryville on the north and Fruitland on the south on Hwy. 61, which roughly parallels I-55. At Uniontown, take Route A east through Frohna to Altenburg. Five miles past Altenburg and one-half mile before the Mississippi River, turn right at the small sign pointing to Tower Rock. The infamous Tower Rock can be spotted about a mile south down this gravel road.

Miss the gravel road to Tower Rock, and the next arrival point is the tiny town of Wittenberg on the Mississippi River. Wittenberg pretty much gave up the ghost after the disastrous flood of 1993.

About the Author

Don Corrigan, an alumnus of the University of Missouri Graduate School of Journalism and Knox College, teaches Environmental Journalism at Webster University, where he has served as a media professor since 1978. At Webster, he has been honored as a Messing Research Scholar, as a Kemper Outstanding Teacher, and as a Presidential Faculty Scholar.

In addition to his academic work, Corrigan is editor and co-publisher of two suburban weeklies in St. Louis, *Webster-Kirkwood Times* and *South County Times*. He has received numerous state and national journalism awards, including a Gannett Foundation Writing Award for Environmental Reporting. He has reported for his newspaper group from Russia, Bosnia, Northern Ireland and Vietnam. He has served on the editorial board of *St. Louis Journalism Review* for 25 years.

Corrigan and his wife, Susanne, live in Sunset Hills with their two children, Brandon and Christa.

About the Artist

E. J. Thias, a graduate of Washington University, studied drawing and sculpture in addition to receiving a degree in architecture. A celebrated architect, Thias found time to prove himself as an artist and teacher. He taught part time at Washington University shortly after graduation and has been tutoring artists at St. Louis Community College at Meramec since 1969.

Thias, also a freelance illustrator, has books and many landmark calendars and prints published of his penciled drawings. His artwork is at the St. Louis Art Museum, Kodner Gallery, McCaughen & Burr Fine Arts, Art Biz Gallery, Mercantile Library at the University of Missouri–St. Louis Campus, St. Louis Community College Library, and in many private collections.

Ed and his wife, Doris, reside in Sunset Hills, Missouri. They have three children, Eric, Linda Sachs, and Nancy Gronemyer.